S. Hrg. 111–764

FINDING COMMON GROUND WITH A RISING CHINA

HEARING

BEFORE THE

COMMITTEE ON FOREIGN RELATIONS
UNITED STATES SENATE

ONE HUNDRED ELEVENTH CONGRESS

SECOND SESSION

JUNE 23, 2010

Printed for the use of the Committee on Foreign Relations

Available via the World Wide Web: http://www.gpoaccess.gov/congress/index.html

U.S. GOVERNMENT PRINTING OFFICE

63–053 PDF   WASHINGTON : 2010

For sale by the Superintendent of Documents, U.S. Government Printing Office
Internet: bookstore.gpo.gov   Phone: toll free (866) 512–1800; DC area (202) 512–1800
Fax: (202) 512–2104   Mail: Stop IDCC, Washington, DC 20402–0001

COMMITTEE ON FOREIGN RELATIONS

JOHN F. KERRY, Massachusetts, *Chairman*

CHRISTOPHER J. DODD, Connecticut
RUSSELL D. FEINGOLD, Wisconsin
BARBARA BOXER, California
ROBERT MENENDEZ, New Jersey
BENJAMIN L. CARDIN, Maryland
ROBERT P. CASEY, JR., Pennsylvania
JIM WEBB, Virginia
JEANNE SHAHEEN, New Hampshire
EDWARD E. KAUFMAN, Delaware
KIRSTEN E. GILLIBRAND, New York

RICHARD G. LUGAR, Indiana
BOB CORKER, Tennessee
JOHNNY ISAKSON, Georgia
JAMES E. RISCH, Idaho
JIM DeMINT, South Carolina
JOHN BARRASSO, Wyoming
ROGER F. WICKER, Mississippi
JAMES M. INHOFE, Oklahoma

DAVID McKean, *Staff Director*
KENNETH A. MYERS, JR., *Republican Staff Director*

(II)

CONTENTS

(III)

FINDING COMMON GROUND WITH A RISING CHINA

WEDNESDAY, JUNE 23, 2010

U.S. SENATE,
COMMITTEE ON FOREIGN RELATIONS,
Washington, DC.

The committee met, pursuant to notice, at 2:38 p.m., in room SD–419, Dirksen Senate Office Building, Hon. John F. Kerry (chairman of the committee) presiding.

Present: Senators Kerry, Casey, Shaheen, Lugar, and Risch.

OPENING STATEMENT OF HON. JOHN F. KERRY, U.S. SENATOR FROM MASSACHUSETTS

The CHAIRMAN. So, this very quiet hearing room will already—will, I should say, come to disorder so we can come to order. [Laughter.]

Everybody's so quiet, it's amazing.

Anyway, welcome. The hearing is now formally open. And I appreciate everybody's patience.

I apologize for being late. We thought we had a couple of votes coming up at 2:30, and I was going to try and vote, and then come and open the hearing. And then, as is probably normal operating procedure here, the votes got put off, and we'll sort of wait to be interrupted, so we'll try to proceed ahead.

So, thank you all, including my good friend and ranking member, Senator Lugar, for your patience and—before we open.

Let me just say, at the top of this hearing, that President Obama has just taken decisive action in accepting the resignation of General McChrystal. And needless to say, I think all of us would have been happier if this distraction, interruption in the mission, had never occurred. I'm confident that there are a lot of folks in General McChrystal's immediate circle who would feel similarly. But, it has happened, and we are where we are. And I applaud the decisive, crisp, swift action that the President took in making the decision. I think it was appropriate that he did that, and I think he made the right decision, to accept the resignation.

I also believe he made the right decision in selecting General Petraeus to take over that command. The President made it clear that no one is above the mission, and he's not going to accept anything less than the unified effort on this mission, within his administration and within the command structure. That's appropriate.

So, I know General Petraeus, as we all do. We have great confidence in him. And he's a proven leader, and I'm confident that the

(1)

skills that he brings as a soldier and as a general—and also as a diplomat—will help to make this transition a smooth transition.

American lives are on the line, and we simply can't afford a moment of distraction. It's time for all of us to be strictly focused on the mission itself.

And this committee will be holding a series of hearings in order to evaluate that mission and keep the American people apprised of where we are, measured against the benchmarks that the committee has previously established.

Today, we are gathered to discuss another important issue, and one that will be with us, in terms of the relationship, throughout this century certainly, probably the single most important relationship that will define a lot of global events over the course of this century, and that is, how we find common ground with a rising China.

We're pleased to welcome two very respected experts: Ambassador Carla Hills and Dr. Laura Tyson. And, I might say, Zbig Brzezinski, former national security advisor of President Carter, was supposed to be here to join us this afternoon, but he had to cancel at the last moment, due to a health issue. But, I am told that he will be fine, and we look forward to welcoming him back here soon.

How the United States, in concert with our friends and allies, responds to China's growing economic might, military capabilities, and political influence will significantly shape the international order of this century.

Just about every global challenge that we face requires cooperation with China. Nuclear proliferation, global economic stability, climate change, just to mention a few. Clearly, building a positive and constructive relationship that can benefit both of our countries and enhance global prosperity and peace for decades to come is a central objective for all of us. That's why the administration has made an energetic effort to manage and to grow the partnership, through the Strategic and Economic Dialogue, as well as dozens of Cabinet-level visits to China.

Still, United States-China relations, it is fair to say, remain a work in progress. We don't always see eye to eye. Our interests sometimes differ, and so do our approaches to shared concerns.

What's more, both countries still mistrust each other's intentions on issues, such as China's defense modernization, the future of Taiwan, and the situation in Tibet. And there is still a great uncertainty about exactly how we will manage our growing economic interdependence.

It's striking how much of the story of United States-China relations remains yet to be written. Looking forward, as China becomes more prosperous and powerful—and it will, absolutely and inevitably—we should not be surprised that it may also become more assertive. The question is how China will use that rising influence to shape global institutions, whether our cooperation can increase as China's stature does, and whether China will agree, or find it necessary and desirable, to take on global responsibilities as its own economic and security interests expand.

This week's announcement on the renminbi is a case in point. China's decision to allow more flexibility in its currency is a welcome step, and many people would argue that it's a long overdue step, toward a rebalancing of the world economy. But, it was the subject of a very heated debate in China itself, and we will need to watch closely to see how vigorously Beijing implements its new policy.

Of the two most important economies of the 21st century, ours is still the largest, China's is growing and will soon be the largest. So, the important question is to see how we can and should compete, but we also need to make certain that that competition takes place on a level playing field.

We need to do more than just talk about difficult issues, such as indigenous innovation schemes, government procurement policies, and protecting intellectual property. We actually need to find meaningful actions between us that make a difference in the leveling of that playing field.

In recent days, we have seen positive steps by China to stop the spread of nuclear weapons. And I think all of us appreciate China's vote for new sanctions against Iran at the United Nations. That's an important cooperative effort and an important measure of China's role in the world today. I hope that China will now join with us and other members of the Security Council in aggressively implementing these sanctions, and also in condemning North Korea's recent aggression against South Korea.

Differences remain, however, and it's impossible to ignore them. We need to work to enhance our strategic dialogue, to increase trust and reach new understandings. And this engagement should include high-level military-to-military talks. And these talks shouldn't be switched off whenever one side perceives some kind of slight, the slight of the moment, if you will, to its particular interests. If we want to build our capacity to manage global crises together, those kinds of talks are even more important when tensions do arise.

Even as we seek common ground with China, we will never abandon our values. We have to continue to encourage China to adhere to international human norms for rights—human rights, labor rights, political rights—and environmental protection. Based on my own conversations with China's top leaders, I believe that our commitment to these values can actually support China's own long-term efforts to build a harmonious society.

And finally, while our companies will inevitably compete in many areas, there are challenges, such as climate change, where our two nations should be collaborating against a shared threat, and where, together, we have the ability to offer leadership to the world.

As today's largest producer of greenhouse gas emissions, and history's largest cumulative emitter of greenhouse gases, China and America have a special responsibility to lead a global effort to reduce emissions, and, particularly, we can work together to develop the clean technologies, the new technologies, the clean and alternative energy sources, of the future. The truth is that no two nations have as much opportunity to set the mark for what we all should be achieving. And if China and the United States engage in this effort, and do so together, it is guaranteed that the rest of the world will follow, and be compelled, ultimately, to do so.

To help us look into the future and navigate the thicket of issues facing America and China, we have two longtime China hands here with us today. Ambassador Carla Hill served as the U.S. Trade Representative under President George H.W. Bush, and she co-chaired the influential Council on Foreign Relations Task Force on China, and currently chairs the National Committee on U.S.-China Relations.

Dr. Laura Tyson is the former chair of the Council of Economic Advisors during the Clinton administration, and the former dean of the London Business School. Dr. Tyson currently serves on President Obama's Economic Recovery Advisory Board, and she is a professor at Berkeley's Haas School of Business.

So, I invite both of our witnesses to feel free to summarize their comments, if they would. We will introduce the full text into the record as if read in full, and we look forward to your testimony. And, again, we're grateful to both of you for being here today.

Senator Lugar.

STATEMENT OF HON. RICHARD G. LUGAR, U.S. SENATOR FROM INDIANA

Senator LUGAR. Mr. Chairman, I join you in welcoming our distinguished witnesses for this important hearing.

China's rising financial and strategic power is a crucial factor in our approach to global economic, energy, and security problems. The United States must come to grips with the incredibly complex set of choices and opportunities that China represents.

China is demanding a greater say in the management of the world economy through the G20 and other mechanisms. Its global leverage has increased as it has positioned itself as the leading creditor nation with more than 20 percent of the world's current account balance surplus.

According to the most recent data, China is the United States Government's largest foreign creditor, holding approximately 23 percent of the $4 trillion we owe to other countries. The Chinese continue to buy United States bonds at a rapid pace, but we cannot count on this continuing indefinitely. Some thought must be given to how we work with China to establish a more sensible global balance that depends less on Chinese credit and demand by American consumers.

The Treasury Department decided to delay publication of the congressionally mandated report on China's international economic and exchange rate policies until after the May 27th Strategic and Economic Dialogue with China and the June 5th G20 meetings. Now that these meetings have concluded, Congress is eager to receive Treasury's assessment.

I look forward to our witnesses's comments on China's recent decision to increase the flexibility of its exchange rate, which the Obama administration has welcomed. Is this a significant step, and can it have a positive impact on the U.S. economy?

China remains an extremely important market for United States exports. Currently, China is our second-largest goods trading partner with more than $407 billion in two-way trade in 2008. Since being admitted to the World Trade Organization in 2001, China has become the United States third-largest export market, accounting for 5.4 percent of total U.S. exports.

But this expansion of trade has not reached its full potential, in part because of impediments to American business activity in China. American businesses and agricultural exporters report that operating in China is becoming more difficult, not less. We are hearing increasingly frequent complaints about inconsistent application of rules, requirements for so-called "indigenous innovation," rising nontariff barriers to trade, inconsistent market access, and lack of enforcement of intellectual property rights.

Civil society within China continues to face immense challenges in promoting rule of law and human rights reform. While the administration and the Congress have been focusing on matters related to currency reform and the China-United States trade imbalance, other issues also warrant concern.

On the military front, since announcement of the Taiwan arms sales, the United States has made attempts to reengage Beijing, including a recent overture by Secretary of Defense Gates on a reciprocal visit to China this June that was rebuffed by China's military.

In East Asia, the United States continues economic sanctions against Burma, while China increases its economic engagement with the military junta. China has been helpful in encouraging Pyongyang to participate in the six-party talks. But at the same time, Beijing is apparently strengthening its assistance to North Korea, even after the sinking of South Korea's ship and the loss of 46 sailors.

China's global advances to secure energy assets and increase its influence are perhaps most intense in its own backyard. China is dedicating massive financial and cultural resources to its neighbors in the region, with implications for traditional United States relations with Asian countries.

Energy security is a strategic interest for both China and the United States. As the New York Times said on June 18, 2010, "as China counts on more years of global leadership in economic growth, global warming remains a secondary concern. Secure sources of energy to fuel that growth are what matter most."

I welcome the Obama administration's high-level attention to energy cooperation with China, which could benefit price stability and may enhance Sino-American cooperation on other international security issues.

While all of this is underway, we must not lose sight of our strategic and economic relationship with Japan. As administration officials pursue new avenues to improve the United States-China relationship, we must maintain and strengthen our ties with Tokyo.

I look forward to the hearing of the testimony of our distinguished witnesses, and our questions and answers.

And I thank you, Mr. Chairman.

The CHAIRMAN. Thank you very much, Senator Lugar.

Dr. Tyson, if you would lead off, and then, obviously, Ambassador Hills.

Thank you very much.

STATEMENT OF LAURA TYSON, FORMER CHAIRPERSON OF THE PRESIDENT'S NATIONAL ECONOMIC COUNCIL (NEC), PROFESSOR, BERKELEY HAAS SCHOOL OF BUSINESS, BERKELEY, CA

Dr. TYSON. Certainly.

The testimony I have submitted was done jointly with Stephen Roach, who is the chairman of Morgan Stanley Asia. I've worked with him for many years on issues of China and Asia.

We focused on some of the policy priorities that were at the center of the most recent Strategic and Economic Dialogue discussions. They were the issues of rebalancing growth in the United States and China; related to that, the exchange rate itself and the policies and issues around the trade barriers that you have mentioned. Let me highlight some of our major recommendations on each of these issues.

First of all, I think it is important to start with the view that I've heard shared by both of you that the Strategic and Economic Dialogue is an important forum in which the United States and China can discuss issues on which they can cooperate and also issues that divide them to come up with solutions.

At the most recent meetings, a major focus of the discussion was global rebalancing. Now, I realize that rebalancing has become a common phrase among economists, but its meaning is not entirely obvious.

At the height of the great credit and export bubble of 2006–07, China was running a current account surplus of around 11 percent, widely viewed to be unsustainable, and the United States was running a current account deficit of about 7 percent, also widely considered to be unsustainable. So, both countries have to get their imbalances down. China has to get its current account surplus down and the United States has to get its current account deficit down. And that to the first approximation, is what "rebalancing" means.

"Rebalancing" also means a change in growth strategies for both the United States and China. China has followed, very successfully, a very aggressive export-led strategy. The Chinese now talk about, and certainly the United States talked with China about, the need to shift their growth strategy to depend more on domestic demand and less on exports.

That's what "rebalancing" means in China; it means bolstering domestic demand, particularly consumption, and relying less on exports.

In the U.S. case, it's actually a bit more unclear what "rebalancing" means. At a macrolevel, the current account deficit reflects the fact that for a very long period of time now, the United States has been spending more than it has been producing as a nation. So to reduce the current account deficit the United States must reduce its spending, particularly its spending on consumption, or increase its production or do some of both. And that's a different kind of challenge than the rebalancing challenge facing China.

Much of our written testimony focuses on the fact that we think China is taking its rebalancing challenge seriously. If you look at its stimulus policies—and it cooperated quite actively with the United States in the G20 on the need for aggressive stimulus they are very much investment-oriented, and, as far as we can tell, the investment is directed to building the center and western regions of the country to enhance development and consumption at home, not to build export capacity for the rest of the world. This is not another export-led investment boom in China; this is an infrastructure-led investment boom to encourage urbanization and move people from the countryside to the city. Building infrastructure in the countryside and moving people to the cities will encourage consumption by providing the rural population with the electricity they need to have sophisticated equipment in their homes and by facilitating their movement from place to place, thereby improving their access to consumer products and services.

So, we believe that the stimulus policies reflect a real commitment, on China's part, to shift away from exports to domestic demand.

We also think that what China is saying about its upcoming 12th 5-year plan reflect rebalancing. China is introducing new health care systems, new social security systems, and new educational systems. These form the social safety net that has been absent, and without such programs, Chinese households have been encouraged to save to cover their own educational, health care, and retirement needs. So, if the Chinese, in fact, build out their new social safety net systems as they plan, Chinese households will save less and consume more, and that will go a long way to rebalancing growth. China is also talking a lot about the need to bolster labor-intensive services as part of the 12th 5-year plan. The United States tends to think of China's export strategy as an employment strategy. But, actually, China's economy has grown much faster than its employment. China's development strategy has actually not been particularly labor-intensive. To boost employment growth, China needs to encourage the development of labor-intensive services and it looks like they're on course to do that.

As a result of these rebalancing policies, we believe that in the future the current account surplus in China will be significantly lower relative to its GDP than it was in 2006 and 2007. It's already significantly down, and we believe it will continue to trend down. And we think that will be a very important contribution by China to the rebalancing part of the United States-China agenda.

As far as the exchange rate is concerned, I will say a few things about that.

First of all, we rewrote some of our testimony over the weekend based on what the Chinese announced; but, in fact, the first draft of our testimony would have suggested that they do, essentially, what they did—that they move back to the managed float exchange-rate regime that they first adopted in July 2005. The regime in place between 2005 to 2008 had a significant effect on the renminbi dollar rate and on the renminbi multilateral trade-weighted exchange rate. There was significant progress on RMB flexibility during that period of time And this time, it looks like the Chinese authorities will allow even more movement of the rate within a broader bank.

We think that China has decided to restore the 2005–08 regime now for a number of reasons, many reasons in their own interest. Frankly, we think China's decision is a win-win situation. From the

United States point of view, this is something we wanted, but it also is something good for the Chinese economy—because they were having trouble with speculative capital flows, with inflationary pressure and with sterilizing the effects of large purchases of dollar assets on China's money supply. All of these challenges become easier to address with an exchange rate which shows some movement over time.

The new currency regime will also support China's rebalancing agenda. The exchange rate is a relative price. And if you adjust the relative price so foreign goods are cheaper, you will actually import more foreign goods. And if you actually make consumers in China wealthier because of the appreciation of the currency, there'll be more demand for domestic production. And that's essential for rebalancing.

So, we think China's decision to restore its 2005–08 exchange rate regime is a constructive step. We think it's a win-win step. And we can talk about the particulars of how they did it.

Let me turn, then, to the trade agenda. I know that Ambassador Hills is going to talk about this in quite a bit of detail. I suspect we agree on all of this.

I am concerned that China's trade and industrial policies of late seem to be changing in ways that reduce the access of foreign producers to China's market. And nontariff barriers not traditional tariffs are a growing problem. So-called indigenous innovation policies to support the development of China's high-tech companies do not use traditional trade policies.

China is not a signatory of the WTO's Government Procurement Agreement. The United States is. China is using preferential government procurement of high-tech products from Chinese companies to support their development. The fact that the stimulus package in the United States contained some controversial "Buy America" provisions was interpreted by some observers in China as a green light for their own preferential procurement practices. In addition to such practices, other nontariff barriers hindering the access of United States companies to China's market include national standards that favor Chinese companies, the lack of inadequate intellectual property protection for foreign producers, and explicit or implicit local content rules. Many United States companies say that they have to locate a significant share of their activity in China to gain access to its market.

I think it is very revealing that access to China's market by United States companies was the first issue highlighted in the documents describing the S&ED meetings. Although the United States was not able to convince the Chinese to drop some of the most troublesome features of their indigenous innovation agenda, the United States did achieve some changes in China's product accreditation procedures that will make it easier for United States companies to bid for government contracts in China. This is an important first step in easing China's indigenous innovation policies. And the United States and China also agreed to ongoing, high-level discussions about trade concerns in high-technology products.

During the S&ED discussions, China also committed to proposing a more robust offer to join the Government Procurement Agreement. I believe that China's participation in this agreement would be a major step toward easing United States-China trade tensions, especially in techology-intensive products.

In our written testimony, we suggest that there's a bargain that can be made between the United States and China. China complains a lot about United States security controls on exports to China. The facts presented in our testimony indicate that such controls have very little effect on United States exports to China. So the United States can cooperate with China on this issue. Moreover, there are several recent studies recommending that the United States can and should ease its security controls on exports not just to China but to our other trading partners in order to bolster United States exports, without compromising United States security interests.

So, as part of a trade deal with China, the United States could ease some of our security restrictions on exports to China. We could also offer to advance the recognition of China as a country with market-economy status in the WTO. China wants this very much. It's scheduled for automatic approval in 2016. The United States can move the date forward. We have been telling the Chinese that we will do so when they do something on their exchange rate. They have now done something by moving back to the 2005–08 managed exchange rate system. Now we can say, "Yes, let's work with you on getting earlier market-economy status. Let's work with you to reduce security controls on U.S. exports. You, in turn, should make a serious proposal to join the Government Procurement Agreement and continue to curb the use of preferential procurement policies to foster indigenous innovation." I think this is an outline of the kind of bargain we might be able to strike in our trade negotiations with China.

Finally, since I've run out of time, just let me add two things.

First, it is very important for the United States to work with our other trading partners in trying to influence China. One of the reasons China moved, this week on the exchange rate is not because we were pressuring the Chinese authorities but because many other G20 nations were doing so well. There is widespread agreement within the G20 that as part of global rebalancing, China needs a more flexible exchange rate system that allows its currency to appreciate over time in response to market forces. Many of China's other trading partners, particularly in Europe, are also concerned about the nontariff barriers that are part of China's indigenous innovation agenda. Whenever we can work with China's trading partners, we need to do that.

Second, I think we should work on forging a new transpacific partnership agreement that can help move the United States back into the center of regional trade negotiations in Asia. During the last few years, many regional and bilateral trade agreements have been signed throughout Asia, and the United States has not been at the table. If the United States becomes the champion of a free trade area for the Asia Pacific through the transpacific partnership, it would give the United States a tremendous opportunity to participate in the benefits of freer trade and investment flows.

And, by the way, on green trade, that is trade related to environmental products and services; remember that APEC itself was the organization that first negotiated a sectoral agreement for free trade in information technology and this agreement was later adopted by nations around the world. APEC might be able to lead again on a sectoral free trade agreement in green goods and services and such an agreement complement our efforts to cooperate with China on solving global environment challenges.

And finally, let me add that our written testimony addresses the question of whether China might adjust its holdings of U.S. Government securities in response to growing tensions in United States-China relations. For example, if the United States pursues a policy the Chinese deem to be an assault on their sovereignty, such as imposing large punitive tariffs on Chinese products to force China to adjust its exchange rate, would China respond by selling a significant amount of these assets, driving the dollar down and interest rates up? We conclude that there is reason to think that they would, that we tend to exaggerate the costs to them of using this form of retaliation and that we tend to underestimate the strength of their nationalist sentiment in response to what they could consider unfair and unwarranted unilateral U.S. pressure. I think we have to keep these conclusions in mind both in military affairs and in economic affairs.

Let me stop there.

[The prepared statement of Dr. Tyson follows:]

JOINT PREPARED STATEMENT OF LAURA TYSON, SK AND ANGELA CHAN PROFESSOR OF GLOBAL MANAGEMENT, HAAS SCHOOL OF BUSINESS, UNIVERSITY OF CALIFORNIA, BERKELEY, CA, AND STEPHEN ROACH, CHAIRMAN, MORGAN STANLEY ASIA

Chairman Kerry, Ranking Member Lugar and distinguished members of the committee, thank you for the opportunity to testify before your committee on this important relationship.

The United States-China economic relationship is the most important bilateral economic relationship in the world. China is the third-largest and the fastest growing major economy in the world. At current growth rates, it will pass Japan later this year and reach the size of the U.S. economy by 2020 or sooner. The United States is China's second-largest export market and China is America's third-largest export market—and has been the fastest growing market for U.S. exports since the late 1990s. China accounted for 18 percent of U.S. imports and for 36 percent of the U.S. trade deficit over 2008–09. China has emerged as the center of a complex global supply chain for manufactured goods in Asia. A significant share of the value of U.S. imports from China represents intermediate inputs and components produced throughout Asia and assembled into final products for export to the us. China is the largest destination for foreign direct investment, much of it from companies headquartered in the us. More than half of all U.S. imports from China come from companies that are partially or completed owned by foreigners, including U.S. companies. This share is significantly higher for U.S. imports of high-technology products like computers and smart phones. And China has $2.4 trillion of foreign exchange reserves, by far the largest such portfolio in the world. Most of these reserves are held in dollars or dollar-denominated assets. China owns about 25 percent of all U.S. Treasury debt held by foreign investors.

China and the United States both reap substantial returns from the large trade and capital flows that link their economies. But these cross-border flows are lopsided: The United States runs a large trade deficit with China and China runs a large trade surplus with the United States; the United States is a debtor and China is a creditor. The United States relies on its deficit with China as a means to satisfy spending of consumers and businesses and China relies on its surplus with the United States as a means to sustain its production and export-oriented economy. The unbalanced nature of these flows complicates the relations between the United States and China and contributes to tensions between them. Despite these tensions, however, both countries are major beneficiaries of globalization and both share interests in promoting a strong global recovery and fostering sustainable and better balanced global growth. The Strategic and Economic Dialogue (S&ED) is an important forum through which the United States and China can ameliorate the tensions in their relationship and cooperate on policies to foster a balanced and prosperous world economy. In addition, the United States and China are cooperating within the G20 and other multilateral institutions and are committed to strengthening these institutions to address shared global challenges.

In this testimony, we examine some of the U.S. policy priorities that were the focus of the most recent S&ED meetings: macroeconomic policies to promote and rebalance global growth; the currency issue—especially in light of recent adjustments in China's exchange rate regime; and policies to reduce barriers to trade. We also assess the possibility that China might sell some of its U.S. Government debt or slow down its purchases of such debt to influence the outcome of a foreign policy dispute with the United States or to retaliate against a U.S. action that China deems to be an assault on its sovereignty. We conclude with recommendations for U.S. policy.

I. UNITED STATES-CHINA COOPERATION TO PROMOTE A STRONG GLOBAL RECOVERY AND SUSTAINABLE BALANCED GROWTH

1. China's Rebalancing Challenge

In recent G20 discussions and in the latest S&ED discussions, China has committed to cooperate with the United States to promote a strong global recovery and to foster more balanced, sustainable global growth. Chinese authorities have adopted ambitious policies that are consistent with this commitment and that have already delivered measurable results. As a result of its unprecedented monetary and fiscal stimulus measures, China recovered more rapidly than expected from the global slowdown in 2009, ending the year with a growth rate of 8.7 percent. China's strong recovery boosted global growth by providing strong demand for exports from the United States and from China's other trading partners. U.S. exports to China have rebounded much more rapidly than overall U.S. exports during the last year and are now about 20 percent above precrisis levels. U.S. exports to China are still growing much more rapidly than U.S. exports to the rest of the world. During the first quarter of 2010, U.S. merchandise exports to China grew by almost 50 percent from year-earlier levels while U.S. exports to the rest of the world grew by about 20 percent. China is now the third-largest and most rapidly growing market for U.S. exports, with double-digit growth across a wide range of U.S. products from high-tech manufactured goods to agricultural goods. Whether China's recent stimulus actions will also deliver on its commitment to foster more balanced future growth, however, is not certain. Faced with a dramatic collapse in China's export markets in the wake of global recession, Chinese authorities had little choice but to reorient their growth policies in the short run. The unprecedented 11.9 percent drop of world merchandise trade in 2009 choked off China's long vigorous export sector. In the short span of 7 months Chinese exports went from boom to bust—a +26 percent year over year increase in July 2008 gave way to a −27 percent decline by February 2009. Real GDP growth screeched to a standstill as measured on a sequential quarterly basis, and over 20 million migrant Chinese workers lost their jobs in export-led Guangdong province. For a nation long fixated on labor absorption and social stability, this was the functional equivalent of China's dreaded recession and called for a massive stimulus response to bolster domestic demand.

Within domestic demand, China's stimulus measures have focused primarily on fixed investment. There are concerns among China's trading partners that this investment is adding excess capacity in manufacturing that will feed another surge of exports—and a renewed widening of China's trade surplus—as the global economy recovers. In fact, most of China's stimulus investment has been directed to massive, multiyear infrastructure projects especially in the western and central regions of the country. (More than 70 percent of China's stimulus package has been devoted to infrastructure projects, Sichuan earthquake reconstruction and public housing projects.) The surge in infrastructure spending in turn has sparked a pickup in private-sector investment by augmenting demand for goods and services provided by private firms, especially those in the manufacturing sector. Rapid growth in investment spending has augmented household income growth, especially in urban areas; moreover, growth in household incomes along with targeted proconsumption incentives for selected consumer durables has supported solid consumption growth.

On the surface, the rebalancing of China's growth toward domestic demand appears to be confirmed by recent data. In 2009, consumption accounted for 4.6 percentage points or about half of China's GDP growth, and in the first quarter of 2010, consumption contributed a record 6.2 percentage points to China's GDP growth. In 2009, China's current account surplus as a share of GDP fell to 6.1 percent, down sharply from its peak of 11 percent in 2007, and dropped further to only about 1 percent of GDP in the first quarter of 2010. China's overall trade surplus as a share of its economy has fallen sharply by about half during the last 2 years.

Some observers express concerns that these trends are temporary and that the rebalancing of China's growth strategy will end when the global economy recovers and global markets for China's exports rebound. In fact, the May trade surplus widened to $19.5 billion from a surplus of $1.7 billion in April and a modest deficit in March. These results are consistent with these concerns and suggest that it may be premature to celebrate the onset of a sustained structural rebalancing of the Chinese economy. But we believe that China's rebalancing is likely to continue over the long term out of both design and necessity. For an externally dependent Chinese economy, the latter motive is especially germane in the post-crisis era—an era that is likely to face lingering headwinds from sluggish demand in the developed world. If there was any doubt about the state of global demand in the aftermath of the global recession in 2009, recent problems in Europe should dispel a false sense of optimism. First, the United States and now Europe—the growth in global final demand that was the sustenance of China's export growth is in serious trouble. And there are compelling reasons to believe that such trouble will not be fleeting—that it will be an enduring feature of the post-crisis environment for several years to some. In order to avoid a sustained shortfall of export-led growth and the social instability it would imply, China needs a new source of growth. And it needs one quickly.

A significant rebalancing of the Chinese economy is really the only answer to China's post-crisis wake-up call. GDP growth needs to shift away from the export- and investment-led dynamic that powered the economy so successfully over the past 30 years toward the sector that has been left behind—internal private consumption. At their peak in early 2007, exports and fixed investment totaled 75 percent of Chinese GDP—more than double the 35-percent share going to private consumption. To some extent, the low share of consumption is the result of high household precautionary saving rates necessitated by the lack of a social safety net—social security, private pensions, medical and unemployment insurance are all lacking for most Chinese citizens. But consumption also has been held back by slow income growth, with wages increasing much more slowly than productivity and rising profits feeding high enterprise saving rates. Enterprises now generate more than half of China's saving.

There are signs that this situation may be changing. There have been recent significant increases (20 percent or more) in minimum wages in key places like Beijing and Guangdong province, and several strikes have ended with sizeable wage increases. The number of young people entering the workforce is slated to decline by almost 30 percent over the next 10 years, and survey evidence indicates that increasingly scarce younger workers may expect higher wages and better working conditions before they are willing to migrate to factory jobs far from their homes. Fully 40 percent of China's population remains in low-productivity agriculture, so there is still a lot of surplus labor. But there are growing signs that the reservation wage for surplus labor is increasing, and this may be another factor that helps rebalance China's future growth.

China's infrastructure-led stimulus policies are building a foundation for strong future growth in domestic consumption through job creation and through projects that not only bolster the development potential of the western and central regions of the country but also reduce physical bottlenecks to rural consumption and rural-urban migration. These are the regions where most of China's surplus labor is located. There is good reason to believe that China will use its upcoming 12th Five-Year Plan (2011–16) to lay out a broad framework to continue this proconsumption rebalancing. The 5-year planning cycle has long been Beijing's principal means for refocusing and redirecting the economy. That purpose seems all the more meaningful in a post-crisis global climate that challenges one of the critical assumptions that has underpinned the export-led growth dynamic for 30 years—the vigor of support from external demand.

China's proconsumption plan is likely to have three major macro goals—to reduce precautionary household saving; to temper widening income disparities; and to uncover new sources of job creation. Each of these goals will require major policy initiatives. On the saving front, it's all about the social safety net—namely social security, private pensions, medical, and unemployment insurance. China has taken only small steps in these areas. It now needs to take big convincing steps in order to reduce the excesses of fear-driven precautionary saving. At the same time, income inequality can only be addressed if China tackles the serious problem of lagging rural incomes—the some 700 to 800 million Chinese who still live at relatively impoverished income levels in the countryside. Several policy initiatives will be required here—especially tax rebates to rural families, rural land and ownership reforms, IT-enabled connectivity of agricultural communities, and ongoing incentives to sustain rural-urban migration, which is essential to boosting agricultural productivity. Finally, on-the-job creation front, China needs a blueprint for the development of large-scale, transactions-intensive services industries such as wholesale and retail trade, domestic transportation, supply-chain logistics, and leisure and hospitality. China needs to shift its development strategy away from laborsaving manufacturing for export toward labor-intensive services for domestic consumption.

If the 12th Five-Year Plan contains half of the initiatives outlined above, we believe that China will make important progress in shifting sustained support of its macroeconomy from external to internal demand. As a share of GDP China's current account surplus has already shrunk from an 11-percent peak in 2007 to slightly over 1 percent in the first quarter of 2010. Although a significant portion of this reduction is cyclical as we noted above, there is good reason to believe that China's external imbalance has peaked and that a consumer-led rebalancing will mean a significantly lower current account surplus in the years ahead.

Nor do we believe that Chinese families are culturally predisposed toward high and rising personal saving—suggesting that this transformation will take decades to occur. With the right incentives and job-creation initiatives, we would not be surprised to see the consumption share of the Chinese economy rise from 35 percent currently to the 42-percent to 45-percent range by 2016—still low by international standards but a major increase from current levels. The key for the 12th Five-Year Plan is to move the needle from the old growth model to the new growth model—setting in motion a powerful rebalancing momentum that will sustain Chinese growth for years to come.

2. The Role of China's Exchange Rate Policies in Global Rebalancing

Exchange rate policy has proved to be a lightening rod in United States-China economic relations in recent years. We applaud China's June 19 announcement to end the crisis-induced repegging of the renminbi-dollar cross-rate which has been in place since July 2008. By returning to the "managed float" foreign exchange regime which it first adopted in July 2005, China has signaled both flexibility and practicality in dealing with a very contentious global issue. Although the full extent of the resulting Chinese currency adjustment is unknown, it should be stressed that this is the same regime that resulted in a 20-percent appreciation of the renminbi versus the dollar in the 3 years ending July 2008. Under the presumption of a sustainable recovery in the global economy, there is good reason to expect that a resumption of gradual RMB appreciation will track a similar trajectory in the years ahead. China should be commended for having taken a very important first step in the right direction.

It was actually an auspicious time for China to act—not just because of mounting global pressure on the eve of the G20 meeting in Toronto but also because market conditions may work in its favor. Recent turbulence in global currency markets caused by the flight from the euro to the dollar, combined with China's reduced trade and current account surplus, gives China an opportunity to reform its currency regime at a time when there is less upward market pressure on the RMB.

China's shift in currency policy also seems well aligned with the broader strategic objectives of the Obama administration. In recent congressional testimony (June 10, 2010), Treasury Secretary Timothy Geithner argued that over time a more flexible market-driven RMB will be good for the global economy because it will facilitate more balanced and sustainable global growth. He also argued that it would serve China's interests because it will support China's rebalancing agenda and because it will enable China to pursue a more independent monetary policy. Secretary Geithner did not argue that greater flexibility in the RMB exchange rate would reduce the U.S. bilateral trade deficit with China. Nor did he call for an appreciation of the RMB. Rather he noted that a stronger RMB as the result of market forces within a more flexible exchange rate system would benefit China and promote global rebalancing. We agree with the conceptual arguments and recommendations made by Secretary Geithner in his written testimony and we applaud his discussion of China's currency policy from a multilateral perspective rather than from a contentious and misleading bilateral one.

In that vein, it is essential to put the currency issue in the context of the world's broader rebalancing imperatives. An RMB-dollar adjustment is not the only option that China has to address its fair share of the global rebalancing agenda. The key challenge for all unbalanced economies—including China and the United States—is to reduce their global imbalances. That is true whether those imbalances take the American form of a saving gap and current account deficit or the Chinese form of a saving excess and a current account surplus.

In the case of China, the structural policies that we suspect are likely to be featured in the upcoming 12th Five-Year Plan could well be far more effective than the more circuitous option of a currency adjustment. It is up to China to decide which of those options—or which combination of them—works best. The rest of the world has a right to insist that China face up to its saving imbalance, but does not have the right to insist on the precise mechanism that China employs to accomplish this task. The same argument, of course, also applies to the tactics and strategy that the United States employs to cut its budget deficit and boost domestic saving. While the rest of the world has a right to insist that America take its rebalancing imperatives seriously, it is the sovereign right of the United States to decide on the best ways to accomplish this objective.

That's not to say there isn't a compelling domestic rationale for China to allow a stronger RMB. Indeed, RMB appreciation would certainly complement China's domestic rebalancing agenda both by boosting the purchasing power of Chinese consumers and by encouraging Chinese producers to shift production away from exports toward domestic markets. Moreover, a stronger currency would temper the impacts of imported inflation—hardly inconsequential in light of China's recent cyclical upsurge in inflation to 3.1 percent in May 2010.

Reforming the exchange rate regime in a way that allows the RMB to appreciate gradually in response to market forces also gives China time to liberalize its capital markets to prepare for greater exchange rate flexibility. We do not endorse the view expressed by many that China should make an immediate large upward adjustment in the RMB-dollar exchange rate. China's June 19 policy pronouncement, which stresses a return to precrisis "floating bands," all but rules out such an action. And with good reason: As a developing economy with a still embryonic financial system, China must continue to focus on financial stability and potential vulnerability to speculative capital flows. For that consideration alone, there is ample justification for China to view a tightly managed band on the dollar-RMB relationship as an important stability anchor.

Bilateral political tensions aside, we agree with Secretary Geithner that it is critical to assess the currency ramifications of global rebalancing from a multilateral perspective. In this regard, it bears noting that on a broad trade-weighted basis, the RMB is up 7 percent (in real terms) from its late 2009 low and up 19 percent from its early 2005 low. In other words, despite the repegging of the RMB to the dollar over the past 2 years, it is factually incorrect to maintain that the RMB has not moved in a broader global context. It is equally important to stress that there are long and uncertain lags associated with the impacts of a shift in relative prices between China and the rest of the world on global imbalances. The example of Japan in the late 1980s raises serious questions about whether a sizeable appreciation of the RMB against the dollar over the next few years would have a sizeable effect on these imbalances. After all, while the yen more than doubled in value relative to the dollar from early 1985 to late 1988, Japan's outsize current account surplus barely budged.

China's decision to return to its precrisis system and allow the RMB to fluctuate against the dollar within a tightly managed band is unlikely to eliminate U.S. concerns about the RMB-dollar exchange rate. A renewed post-crisis rebound of Chinese exports, in conjunction with sluggish U.S. job growth and unacceptably high unemployment, has fueled congressional frustrations about the persistence of a large bilateral trade deficit with China. As a result, pressures on China for a major RMB revaluation—or for the U.S. Treasury to name China as a currency manipulator if that doesn't occur—have intensified. Many Members of Congress believe that a sizeable RMB appreciation relative to the dollar would be an effective way to ease the plight of America's beleaguered middle class. They also believe that if China does not act voluntarily to relieve those pressures, the United States should take offsetting action. At least, China's June 19 adjustment of its currency policy sends an important signal to U.S. policymakers that the Chinese leadership takes these concerns seriously.

Unfortunately, a significant appreciation of the RMB-dollar exchange rate—or the countervailing trade sanctions that might occur in its absence—might well backfire. Much of the growth in U.S. imports from China has been the result of production moving to lower cost China not from the United States but from other higher cost foreign countries especially in Asia. China has become the center of a global supply chain that enhances efficiency, keeps production costs down and supplies U.S. consumers with attractively priced products, purchased in large amounts by low- and middle-income families. A significant share of the value of U.S. imports from China represents the value of components produced in other countries and assembled in China for sale in the United States. China's share of the value-added for some products may be only 20–30 percent of the total value of U.S. imports from China.

Tariffs imposed on Chinese exports to the United States in an effort to offset the so-called RMB currency subsidy would raise the prices of these products for U.S. consumers and drive their production not back to the United States but to other emerging market countries, reducing the efficiencies of the supply chain and increasing production costs. The increase in prices on U.S. imports that resulted would be the functional equivalent of a tax hike on both U.S. companies and American consumers.

Moreover, there are other equally serious analytical pitfalls to a bilateral assessment of the China problem. Yes, China accounts for the largest piece of America's trade deficit—some 36 percent of the average merchandise trade gap over 2008–09. But the key point to stress here is that the United States had trade deficits with over 90 countries during the same period—a multilateral imbalance that stems from the unprecedented shortfall in U.S. saving discussed below. Lacking its own saving, the only way for the United States to keep growing is to import surplus saving from abroad and run a large current account and multilateral trade deficit in order to attract foreign capital. The Chinese piece may account for the largest share of this multilateral imbalance but that is more likely traceable to conscious outsourcing decisions of U.S. multinationals and strong consumer preferences for low-cost, high-quality goods made in China than to unfair trading practices. The bottom line is that America's multilateral trade imbalance cannot be addressed by putting pressure on a bilateral foreign exchange rate with China.

Finally, it is important to emphasize that if the U.S. Congress were to impose trade sanctions on imports from China, it is highly likely that China would retaliate. That retaliation could take one of three forms: lodging a WTO complaint; imposing tit-for-tat trade sanctions on U.S. exports to China; or reducing demand for U.S. Government securities. The latter two options would hardly be inconsequential for the United States. Tariffs on U.S. exports to China would hit America's third-largest export market—a serious problem for the Obama administration's goal of doubling U.S. exports over the next 5 years. Similarly, reduced Chinese buying of U.S. Treasuries would be highly problematic for the funding of the Federal deficit at attractive interest rates and could trigger a spike in U.S. interest rates, a sharp drop in the dollar's value and renewed instability in global financial markets. (The possibility that China might respond to U.S. pressure on its exchange rate policy by adjusting its demand for U.S. Treasuries is discussed below.)

3. The U.S. Rebalancing Challenge

Rebalancing growth was a major topic at the recent S&ED meetings and U.S. officials agreed on the need to rebalance growth of the American economy away from consumption and large Federal Government deficits toward higher household saving rates, greater reliance on exports and investment, and sustained deficit reduction. U.S. officials emphasized the Obama administration's multiyear plan to achieve $1 trillion in deficit reduction over the next decade. The plan includes freezing nonsecurity discretionary spending for 3 years, reducing defense spending in Iraq and Afghanistan, and allowing the 2001–2003 tax cuts for households earning more than $250,000 to expire. According to the administration's latest projections, this plan would reduce the deficit from 10.6 percent of GDP in 2010 to 3.9 percent by 2015, a record 5-year reduction that would occur despite an average unemployment rate of 7.9 percent during the period. If adopted, this plan would be a significant step toward rebalancing the U.S. economy, but it would leave the United States with a projected average deficit of 3.9 percent of GDP between 2015 and 2020, and it would not stabilize the federal debt to GDP ratio, which would continue to rise through 2020 and beyond. As long as the debt to GDP ratio is rising, U.S. fiscal policy is not on a sustainable long-run path. This could prove problematic for global investors, including the Chinese, who are currently willing to purchase U.S. Government debt at interest rates that are at or below historical averages.

During the S&ED discussions, U.S. officials assured their Chinese counterparts that the Obama administration is committed to reducing the deficit to 3 percent of GDP and stabilizing the debt to GDP ratio by 2015. President Obama has created a special bipartisan National Commission on Fiscal Responsibility and Reform charged with the task of proposing additional spending cuts and/or revenue increases to bring the primary budget deficit into balance and thereby stabilize the debt to GDP ratio in that year. Primary balance requires that total Federal Government spending excluding interest payments on the debt, equal total Federal Government revenues. According to the administration's latest projections, the primary deficit will be around $174 billion in 2015; by contrast, according to the most recent Congressional Budget Office projections, the primary deficit will exceed $250 billion in that year, and many private sector projections are even larger.

A recent study by the Center for American Progress (CAP) found that closing a primary budget gap of $250 billion in 2015 by spending cuts alone would require a cut of almost 7 percent in every area of federal spending, except interest payments on the debt. If cuts in Social Security spending, additional cuts in Medicare and Medicaid spending beyond those in the health care reform, and additional cuts in defense spending beyond those in the President's budget are excluded, balancing the primary budget by spending cuts alone would require a 16-percent cut in the rest of government spending. CAP estimates that closing the primary budget gap by revenue increases alone would require a 7.3-percent increase in all federal taxes and fees. If those making less than $250,000 a year are excluded, taxes and fees collected from those making more than $250,000 a year and from U.S. corporations would have to increase by almost 25 percent. These calculations make it very clear that balancing the primary budget by 2015 will require some combination of very painful spending cuts and revenue increases.

The Commission is charged with making recommendations in December 2010. Given the size of the fiscal problem and the highly charged partisan atmosphere—a climate that may well worsen after the November elections—it is unlikely that the Commission will be able to agree on major recommendations and that such recommendations will be adopted by Congress. So even though the deficit as a share of GDP is likely to decline significantly as the economy recovers and as temporary stimulus and recovery measures die out, the United States will face significant challenges to deliver on its commitment of rebalancing the U.S. economy through fiscal consolidation.

Rebalancing U.S. growth also requires more than a sustainable fiscal path. It also requires reducing the gap between the growth of spending and the growth of income in the United States, and this requires an increase in national saving. America's net national saving rate—the sum total of deprecation-adjusted savings of households, businesses, and the government sector—turned negative in 2008 before plunging to a record low of −2.6 percent of national income in 2009. This is the most serious shortfall of domestic saving by a leading nation in modern history. Just as China must reduce its saving surplus to deliver on its rebalancing commitments, the United States must reduce its saving gap to do the same. Between 2000 and 2008, U.S. saving declined both because of increases in the federal budget deficit—a measure of government disserving—and because of a dramatic drop in household saving. During the recession, the household saving rate has recovered somewhat, rising from essentially zero in 2007 to about 4 percent in 2008–2009 before falling back to about 3.6 percent in April 2010. Many economists predict that the household saving rate will rise during the next several years to its historical average of about 7 percent, but there is considerable uncertainty about this. In the S&ED discussions, the United States promised to introduce policies to reinforce rising household saving rates but did not offer any specifics, and policies tried in the past have not been very effective.

As part of its rebalancing agenda, the administration has also set a goal to double U.S. exports over the next 5 years and has introduced supporting policies and organizational changes. An active U.S. trade policy to reduce access barriers to U.S. exports in rapidly growing emerging markets including China is essential to realizing this goal. We discuss trade policy in United States-China relations in the next section of this testimony. Unfortunately, since Europe is a major destination for U.S. exports and since European companies are major competitors of U.S. companies in China and other rapidly growing export markets, the recent slowdown in Europe and the sharp drop in the value of the euro pose serious downside risks to strong U.S. export growth over the next few years.

Nor would such growth ensure a sustained reduction in the U.S. trade deficit and current account deficit as the economy recovers. The size of these deficits depends on both exports and imports and reflects the size of the U.S. saving gap, or the gap between how much the U.S. produces and how much it spends. During the recession, this gap, as measured by the current account deficit as a share of GDP, declined significantly to 2.9 percent in 2009 from its 2007 peak of 6 percent of GDP. This drop in the saving gap is primarily the result of a sharp reduction in private sector spending relative to private sector income, as U.S. households and businesses have curtailed spending to rebuild balance sheets and deleverage their financial positions. Despite the retrenchment in private sector spending relative to income, the current account deficit, which is a measure of the national saving gap, has remained sizeable because the government deficit has increased as a result of tax cuts and spending increases to combat the recession.

Most forecasters predict that the United States will continue to run a significant current account deficit around 3 percent of GDP for the next several years if the fiscal deficit is reduced and if the household saving rate increases from its historic lows of the 2002–2007 period. A deficit of this size would roughly stabilize foreign U.S. debt as a share of GDP. Provided the United States convinces China and other global investors of its commitment to a sustainable long-term fiscal path, it is likely that the United States can finance a current account deficit of this size with reasonable long-term interest rates on U.S. Government debt in the 4–5-percent range.

What happens to the U.S. trade and current account deficits and to U.S. borrowing requirements from the rest of the world depends primarily on what the United States does to increase private saving and to reduce government dissaving. China's trade and exchange rate policies are of second-order importance. If the United States fails to sustain a significant reduction in its saving gap, its trade and current account deficits will rise again as a share of GDP as the economy recovers. That will be the case even if China succeeds with its own rebalancing agenda and reduces its current account surplus as a share of its GDP and even if China moves to a pure market-determined exchange rate. The risk in this case would be that of an "asymmetrical global rebalancing"—a scenario in which China makes more progress in transitioning to a consumer-led economy than the United States makes in closing its saving gap.

The odds of an asymmetrical rebalancing scenario should not be minimized. China's stimulus policies and the likely components of the 12th Five-Year Plan indicate that China could well make significant progress in rebalancing its economy over the next several years. In contrast, the stimulus policies in the United States, while essential and justifiable to combat the recession, have exacerbated the long-run saving gap and have not rebalanced growth away from consumption toward exports and investment. Moreover, given the partisan atmosphere in Congress, passage of a credible multiyear deficit reduction plan to reduce the Nation's saving gap on a sustained basis once the economy has recovered seems unlikely, at least in the near future.

II. AN ACTIVIST TRADE POLICY TO LEVEL THE PLAYING FIELD IN CHINA AND SUPPORT U.S. REBALANCING

China is now the largest exporter and the third-largest importer in the world. It is the third-largest and fastest growing market for U.S. exports in a wide range of products. If the United States is to succeed in rebalancing its growth—shifting from credit-driven consumption and housing toward investment and exports—continued rapid growth in U.S. exports to China is essential. China also receives a major share of the foreign direct investment of U.S. multinational companies, many of which have extensive and growing operations there. Offshore Chinese production platforms are critical to efficiency solutions for high-cost U.S. manufacturers and support their production, employment, profits, R&D and investment in the us. Access to China's large and growing market is a significant factor in the success of many U.S. businesses, both large multinational companies and many small- and medium-sized companies as well. Reducing barriers that impede the access of U.S. companies to China's markets is and should be a major objective of U.S. trade policy. The Obama administration rightly accorded priority to this goal in the recent S&ED discussions, focusing in particular on the effects of China's innovation policies, government procurement policies, and foreign direct investment policies on American companies exporting to and/or producing in China.

During the last few years, many American companies (along with European and Japanese companies) have raised concerns about China's so-called "indigenous innovation" policies to promote the development of Chinese owned technology and intellectual property and to reduce China's dependence on foreign technologies. Initially, the call for indigenous innovation was more hortatory than real. But recently the call has been given practical effect through policies that include not only strong incentives for innovation by Chinese companies but also policies that discourage the participation of foreign companies in technologies or sectors deemed to be strategic by the Chinese Government. In a recent survey of 388 U.S. companies conducted by the American Chamber of Commerce in China, 28 percent said that they are already losing business as a result of China's indigenous innovation policies, and 57 percent of high-tech companies said that they expect to lose more business in the future as these policies are fully implemented.

Seven of the eight top challenges to doing business in China identified by the survey's respondents relate to obstacles posed by the policies of the Chinese Government in a wide range of areas, including procurement, standard setting, intellectual property protection, subsidies and approvals for foreign direct investment. These survey results reveal a growing concern among American businesses that China is adopting more restrictive promotional policies that favor Chinese companies and that pose significant access barriers to foreign companies doing business in China.

There is mounting evidence that China's trade and industrial policies are changing in ways that are impeding access of foreign producers to China's market and that fall outside of WTO rules and enforcement procedures.

Preference in government procurement has recently become a key weapon in China's arsenal of indigenous innovation policies. According to China's long-term plan for scientific and technological development, the government should establish a priority procurement policy for important high-tech products and equipment developed "by domestic enterprises with independent intellectual property." Since China is not a signatory to the Government Procurement Agreement (GPA) of the WTO, its procurement procedures are not covered by the agreement and not actionable at the WTO. But China's preferential treatment of its domestic producers in government procurement is not an isolated development. Indeed, China's preferential procurement policies were given an implicit green light in 2009 when several nations that are GPA signatories framed their stimulus actions to provide support to their own companies and workers. (The "Buy America" provisions of the U.S. stimulus package are a case a point. Although these provisions did not have a significant effect on procurement and trade in the us, they did send a strong signal to China.)

In November 2009, several of China's most powerful ministries issued a joint circular, announcing the intent to create a national catalogue of "indigenous innovation" products for government procurement," and proposing accreditation conditions to determine whether particular products qualified for inclusion in the catalogue. Although the accreditation conditions do not include explicit restrictions against the products of foreign-owned companies, they effectively deny access to such products if the technology does not originate in China—even if the products are entirely produced in China, with 100 percent local content. That's because most of the products sold by American companies in China embody many technologies sourced from the United States and other locations and also because American companies are reluctant to develop technologies in China as a result of inadequate intellectual property protection there.

We are encouraged that the recent S&ED discussions made some progress on the indigenous innovation and related government procurement issues, although China did not agree to a U.S. request for full suspension of its indigenous innovation policy. Instead, China confirmed its commitment to innovation policies consistent with the principles of nondiscrimination, intellectual property protection and market competition and agreed to hold high-level bilateral talks on such policies. China also agreed that the terms of technology transfer should be shaped by agreements among companies without government interference. In response to U.S. concerns, China removed several troubling conditions from its product accreditation circular, including the requirement that products be patented or trademarked in China, and agreed to delay final implementation of the national catalogue to assess public comments.

China also promised to submit a revised offer to join the WTO Government Procurement Agreement by July. Given the importance of the government and of state-owned companies in the Chinese economy, China's participation in this agreement should be a major objective of U.S. trade policy. As part of its WTO accession agreement, China committed that state-owned and state-invested companies would make their decisions solely on commercial considerations and that the government would not attempt to influence these decisions either directly or indirectly. In principle, these commitments are enforceable through the WTO dispute settlement mechanism. But U.S. companies frequently complain that the procurement decisions of state-owned companies either follow the decisions of state agencies or are influenced by government actors. A convincing bid by China to join the GPA could help assuage these concerns.

In response to Chinese concerns, the United States softened its position on two key issues of longstanding interest to China. First, the United States promised to ease restrictions on some high-technology exports to China. While this is a priority issue for China, U.S. controls on such exports have only a small effect on U.S. trade with China. According to recent estimates, only about 0.3 percent of all U.S. exports to China and about 0.6 percent of all U.S. advanced technology exports to China require an export license. The figures for Europe are comparable: 0.2 percent of all U.S. exports and 0.4 percent of all U.S. advanced technology exports to the EU require a license. Moreover, around 80 percent of the exports to China that require a license receive a license exemption and the value of all denied licenses is minimal. Second, the United States agreed to consult with China on its desire to be accorded "market economy status" within the WTO and scheduled consultations for the fall meeting of the United States-China Joint Commission on Commerce and Trade. In its original accession agreement to the WTO, China agreed to be treated as a non-market economy in antidumping and countervailing duty cases. As a result, the United States or any other WTO member can initiate an antidumping investigation against Chinese products using the product prices of a third country as a benchmark. This makes Chinese firms especially vulnerable to antidumping cases and the imposition of antidumping tariffs on its products. As part of its WTO accession, China also agreed to annual compliances reviews of its implementation of its accession agreement.

So far, the United States has been reluctant to recognize China's status as a market economy and has posed several conditions that China must meet including the adoption of a market-based exchange rate regime. Now the United States will have to decide whether China's decision to allow the market to determine the RMB-dollar rate within a managed band satisfies this condition. We think it should and we think it sets the grounds for progress on China's bid for market access status during the upcoming JCCT consultations. The United States will lose its ability to use the market access issue as a bargaining chip with China in 2016 when it will be accorded such status automatically.

Both the United States and China have been major beneficiaries of the growth in world trade and foreign direct investment triggered by the WTO and both have been active users of WTO enforcement to address trade disputes, including bilateral disputes. In recent testimony, Alan Wolff, cochair of Dewey & LeBoeufs International Trade Practice Group, examined the history of United States-China trade relations within the WTO and concluded that the United States has enjoyed "reasonably positive results." The United States has brought WTO cases against China when the U.S. Government has the support of the relevant businesses or industries and when it believes it can persuade a WTO panel that China is violating its WTO obligations. China has often ceased the practices in question without going through a formal dispute settlement panel process.

But the future is likely to be more challenging because many of the practices at the center of United States-China trade frictions and many of the promotional policies playing a more prominent role in China's development strategy are either inadequately covered or are difficult to enforce by the WTO. These practices include indigenous innovation policies, discriminatory procurement behavior by state-owned enterprises, national standards that favor national champions, lax enforcement of intellectual property protection and implicit or explicit local content rules for participating in major economic sectors like wind and other renewable energies. Such practices are a violation of the spirit and in some instances the law of China's WTO commitments and harm not just U.S. companies but companies from other developed and emerging market nations. That's why the United States should continue to treat market access barriers as a priority issue in the S&ED discussions, should continue to lodge WTO cases against such barriers when they violate China's WTO commitments, and should encourage China's other trading partners to address such barriers in regional and multilateral discussions.

III. CHINA'S HOLDINGS OF UNITED STATES DEBT AND UNITED STATES-CHINA RELATIONS

As of April 2009, China's held over US$2.4 trillion in foreign exchange reserves, by far the largest in the world. Its holdings of U.S. Treasury debt totaled $900 billion, or about 11 percent of total UST debt held by the public and about 25 percent of total UST debt held by foreign investors. (China also holds around $405 billion or about 6 percent of U.S. agency debt, primarily Fannie Mae and Freddie Mac debt). At current trends, even with continued rebalancing in China and smaller current account surpluses as a share of GDP, China's FX reserves will continue to grow, albeit at a slower pace, and are likely to top $3 trillion by 2011. Given the lack of attractive nondollar currency alternatives, exacerbated by the uncertainty and turbulence in euro-denominated assets, it is likely that a significant share of China's growing reserves will continue to be held in U.S. Government securities. And even if there is a sustained increase in U.S. private saving and a significant reduction in the federal budget deficit—both of which are far from certain—it is highly likely that the United States will continue to run a significant current account deficit in the 3-percent to 4-percent range and will continue to depend on foreign investors, including China, to finance its saving gap. Moreover, given the sheer size of China's holdings of U.S. dollars and government securities, a precipitous action by China to shift out of U.S. dollar assets could cause a sizeable increase in long-term interest rates in the United States, and a sharp decline in the prices of U.S. Government securities and the dollar's value. Even cutting the share of China's holdings of U.S. Treasury securities by 5-percentage points would probably be enough to rock global financial markets, with damage on both the United States and China. China would sustain capital losses on its large dollar holdings as a result of falling prices on U.S. Government securities and a drop in the dollar's value.

Despite the prospect of such capital losses, would China be willing to sell some of its dollar holdings to respond to a foreign policy dispute with the United States or to retaliate against what it deemed to be an assault on its sovereignty? For example, if the United States enacted broad-based trade sanctions on China's exports because China does not succumb to U.S. pressure for a sizeable RMB appreciation, would China retaliate by selling some of its stock of U.S. Government assets or reducing its future purchases of such assets? Many observers believe that China would not take such actions, at least not on a meaningful scale, because they would impose painful capital losses on China. Even if such losses were significant, however, China might be willing to bear them in retaliation for what it perceives to be unfair trade or other policy sanctions that infringe on its sovereignty. There is every reason to believe that China would view such U.S. actions as an act of economic aggression. Nationalist sentiment inside of China is very high—suggesting that Beijing would be under considerable pressure to take retaliatory measures irrespective of any potential portfolio losses. There is far more to China's FX management objectives than simply seeking optimal rates of financial return.

Moreover, as Professor Eswar Prasad explained in recent testimony before the United States-China Economic and Security Review Commission, the potential for losses in the value of China's foreign exchange reserves could prove to be quite modest for three reasons:

1. A spike in U.S. interest rates in response to a selloff of U.S. assets by China would impose a capital loss on the value of China's U.S. Treasury holdings on a mark to market basis. But given its large stock of reserves and the fact that it has no obvious liquidity needs, it is likely that China values its assets on a hold to maturity approach rather than a mark to market approach.

2. A decline in the value of the dollar against other major currencies triggered by China's action would reduce the RMB value of China's dollar-denominated holdings, if the RMB appreciated relative to the dollar. Otherwise, China would suffer capital losses on the value of its euro and yen assets as the dollar declined, but it would benefit from enhanced competitiveness if the RMB declined with the dollar against the currencies of its other major trading partners.

3. A sizeable appreciation of the RMB against the dollar would lead to a sizeable capital loss on the value of China's dollar holdings measured in local currency. But the loss could be offset over time as China moves forward on exchange rate flexibility, capital market liberalization, and reserve currency status.

Prasad concludes that a threat by China to move away from U.S. Treasuries is a credible threat that should be taken seriously by U.S. policymakers. We agree. And under current market conditions, such a threat could trigger investor concern about the huge financing needs of the U.S. Government, causing a sharp spike in interest rates and a crisis of confidence in U.S. sovereign debt.

China has repeatedly expressed its desire for FX portfolio diversification—namely, to put in place a disciplined program to reduce its existing holdings of U.S. Government securities and to slow down the acquisition of new holdings. It has been attempting to do this in part through the establishment of the China Investment Corporation, a sovereign wealth fund with an initial capital base of $200 billion. But this is a small amount relative to China's overall dollar holdings. The real problem for China is that there are no relatively safe investments other than U.S. Government bonds that are deep and liquid enough to absorb a significant share of the massive inflow of dollars that enter China each year as a result of its large trade surplus, inward foreign direct investment and hot money in anticipation of a significant RMB appreciation. And the dollar-recycling strategy is, of course, heavily dependent on Beijing's desire to maintain a relatively tight relationship between the RMB and the dollar. Overall, that means that China is likely to continue to hold large amounts of dollar assets and that these holdings will grow each year by a sizeable amount.

IV. RECOMMENDATIONS

The S&ED is an important forum through which the United States and China can ameliorate the tensions in their relationship and cooperate on policies to foster a balanced and prosperous world economy.

The United States should continue to cooperate with China in the G20 on macroeconomic policies to support a strong global recovery and to foster more balanced global growth in the future.

China's stimulus policies fostered a strong rebound of the Chinese economy and boosted global growth by providing strong demand for exports from the United States and China's other trading partners in 2009 and through the first half of 2010. China's stimulus policies helped rebalance China's growth away from dependence on exports and toward domestic demand. In 2009, consumption growth accounted for about half of China's GDP growth and China's current account surplus as a share of its GDP declined by nearly 50 percent.

We recommend that China continue to rebalance its future growth in order to increase the contribution of consumption and to reduce the contribution of exports, and we believe that China will do so out of both necessity and choice. The likelihood of slower consumption growth in both Europe and the United States over the next several years will mean slower growth in the demand for China's exports. To preserve social stability, on which the legitimacy of its leadership depends, China must boost domestic demand to absorb its growing labor force, to move surplus labor from low-productivity agriculture to higher productivity manufacturing and services, and to reduce rural-urban income gaps.

We believe that China's infrastructure-led stimulus policies are building the foundation for strong future growth in domestic consumption. We also recommend and expect that China's upcoming 12th Five-Year Plan will spur accelerated proconsumption rebalancing through investments in China's social safety net, through policies to promote services industries and through tax and other policies to reduce urban-rural income inequality.

We believe that as a result of its consumption-led rebalancing, China's multilateral trade and current account surpluses will be significantly lower as a share of GDP in the future than they were in the peak years of 2006–2008.

China's exchange rate should be assessed from a multilateral perspective rather than from a bilateral, dollar-centric perspective.

We applaud China's June 19 decision to end its crisis-induced RMB-dollar fixed peg and return to the "managed float" foreign exchange regime it first adopted in July 2005. A more flexible RMB driven by market forces benefits the global economy because it facilitates more balanced, sustainable global growth. It is also in China's interest because it supports China's rebalancing goals and it allows China to pursue a more independent monetary policy. At the same time, a tightly managed band on the dollar-RMB exchange rates is an important stability anchor for China's transition to more open capital markets. China's decision to return to a more flexible currency regime and allow the RMB-dollar rate to move within a managed band will allow the RMB to appreciate gradually in response to market forces. Over time, a stronger RMB will contribute to China's rebalancing by boosting the purchasing power of Chinese consumers and by encouraging Chinese producers to shift production toward domestic demand and away from exports.

We do not endorse the view that China should make a large adjustment in the RMB-dollar rate at this time. The RMB has already appreciated significantly in real terms on a multilateral trade-weighted basis. The key imperative for China is to reduce its saving surplus and rebalance its macrostructure. Proconsumption policy initiatives will be more important than changes in the RMB's trade-weighted exchange rate in achieving these goals. The United States should refrain from making explicit demands about how China should go about implementing its rebalancing agenda. In particular, the choice between proconsumption structural adjustments and the RMB-dollar exchange rate should be left to China.

A significant appreciation of the RMB relative to the dollar will not have a significant effect on the U.S. trade deficit or on U.S. employment. Much of the growth in U.S. imports from China has been the result of production moving to lower cost China not from the United States but from other higher cost countries, especially in Asia. And China's bilateral trade deficit with the United States needs to be seen as but one piece of a much broader multilateral problem, reflecting America's large saving gap.

The United States should not impose tariffs on Chinese exports if there is not a significant appreciation of the RMB. Such tariffs would drive production to other emerging market economies not to the United States. In addition, China would retaliate in one of three ways all of which would be damaging to U.S. interests: lodging a WTO complaint that would almost certainly prove successful; imposing tit-for-tat tariffs on U.S. exports to China; or reducing demand for U.S. securities.

Section 3004 (b) of the Omnibus Trade and Competitiveness Act of 1988, which requires the Treasury to issue a biannual foreign exchange report assessing whether U.S. trading partners are "manipulating" their exchange rates vis-a-vis the dollar, has become dangerously politicized and should be repealed or revised. Currency values should be assessed on a multilateral basis rather than a bilateral basis, and the International Monetary Fund, rather than the U.S. Treasury, is the appropriate multilateral organization for evaluating the exchange rate policies of member countries.

The U.S. current account deficit is the result of the Nation's saving gap or the gap between how much the United States is producing and how much it is spending.

To reduce this gap, the United States must reduce the federal budget deficit and, as the economy recovers, must increase the household saving rate, which fell to nearly zero during the 2001–2007 period. A higher household saving rate will require that the United States rebalance growth away from consumption toward reliance on exports and investment.

During the recession, the U.S. saving gap has declined relative to GDP, primarily as a result of a sharp temporary increase in private saving as households and businesses deleverage. But the saving gap has remained substantial as a result of stimulus policies that have caused a big increase in "dissaving" by the Federal Government. What happens to the U.S. current account deficit in the future as the economy recovers depends on what the United States does to reduce its saving gap. China's trade and exchange rate policies are of second-order significance. If the United States fails to reduce this gap, its trade and current accounts deficits will rise again as a share of GDP even if China succeeds in rebalancing its economy.

The possibility of an asymmetrical global rebalancing scenario remains a very real risk. China's stimulus policies and the likely proconsumption thrust of the upcoming 12th Five-Year Plan indicate that China should make significant progress in rebalancing its economy over the next several years. In contrast, the stimulus policies in the United States, although essential and justifiable to offset the 2008–2009 recession, have exacerbated the long-run saving gap and have not rebalanced growth from consumption toward exports and investment. And given the partisan atmosphere in Congress, passage of a credible multiyear deficit reduction plan to reduce the saving gap on a sustained basis once the economy has recovered seems unlikely—at least in the near future.

According to projections by the OMB, the CBO, and private forecasters, U.S. fiscal policy is not on a sustainable path: in the absence of additional deficit reduction policies, the Federal Government's debt will continue to rise relative to GDP through 2020 even if the economy recovers from the 2008–2009 recession.

At the S&ED discussions, the United States committed to adopting policies to achieve fiscal sustainability in the medium to long run and to stabilize the debt-to-GDP ratio. Given the size of projected Federal Government deficits, these policies will require some combination of painful spending cuts and revenue increases. We recommend that the Congress work with the administration to pass a credible multiyear deficit reduction plan to stabilize the debt to GDP ratio. This plan should take effect gradually as the economy recovers: policies to reduce the deficit too quickly will slow the recovery and increase the losses in potential output from high unemployment and excess capacity.

Access to China's large and growing market is a significant factor in the success of many U.S. businesses, both large multinational companies and many small- and medium-sized companies as well. Reducing barriers that impede the access of U.S. companies to China's markets is and should continue to be a major objective of U.S. trade policy.

China's industrial policies appear to be changing in ways that are reducing access of foreign producers to China's market and that fall outside of WTO rules and enforcement procedures. Indigenous innovation policies, discriminatory procurement behavior by state agencies and state-owned enterprises, national standards that appear to favor national champions, lax enforcement of intellectual property protection, and implicit or explicit local content rules in strategic activities like renewable energy are areas of growing concern to U.S. companies. The United States should continue to negotiate with China to reduce these barriers both in the S&ED discussions and in regional and multilateral discussions that include China's other trading partners who are also disadvantaged by such barriers.

Given the importance of the government and of state-owned companies in the Chinese economy, China's participation in the Government Procurement Agreement (GPA) of the WTO should be a major objective of U.S. trade policy. The United States should negotiate with China to ease U.S. security controls on exports to China and to advance the timing for the recognition of China's market economy status in the WTO (currently scheduled for 2016) in return for a strong offer by China to join the GPA. A bargain along these lines could also help revitalize the Doha talks, something the United States and China committed to do at the recent S&ED meeting.

The United States should take the lead in negotiating a Trans-Pacific Partnership agreement as a major step to the creation of a free trade area for the Asia Pacific. Several bilateral and regional preferential trading agreements have recently been signed in Asia, and the region is heading toward the de facto creation of an economic bloc that would be discriminatory against the United States. The completion of a Trans-Pacific Partnership agreement would arrest this disturbing trend and could re-ignite APEC's role in global trade liberalization. In the 1990s, APEC played a key role in the negotiation of a global agreement liberalizing trade in information technology products. A revitalized APEC could play a similar role in the creation of a global agreement on trade in "green" technologies and products.

A threat by China to shift the allocation of its vast foreign exchange reserve portfolio away from U.S. securities to respond to a foreign policy dispute with the United States or to retaliate against a U.S. policy deemed to be an assault on China's sovereignty is a credible threat that should be taken seriously. Even the suggestion of such a move could trigger concerns among global investors about the huge financing needs of the U.S. Government, causing a sharp spike in interest rates, a crisis of confidence in U.S. sovereign debt, and a collapse in the dollar. As the world's largest external borrower, the United States must exercise great caution in exerting undo pressure on its most important foreign lender.

References

Michael Linden and Michael Ettlinger, "Restoring Fiscal Balance: The new Deficit Commission's 2015 Targets, Center for American Progress," April 26, 2010.

Eswar Prasad, "The U.S.-China Economic Relationship: Shifts and Twists in the Balance of Power," written testimony, hearing on "U.S. Debt to China: Implications and Repercussions," U.S.-China Economic and Security Review Commission, February 25, 2010.

Stephen S. Roach, "Consumer-Led China," a paper presented to the 11th annual China Development Forum, sponsored by the Development Research Center of the State Council PRC, held in Beijing on March 20–22 2010.

Stephen S. Roach, "America's China Complex," American Review, May 2010.

Alan W. Wolff, "China in the WTO," written testimony, hearing on "Evaluating China's Role in the World Trade Organization over the Past Decade," U.S.-China Economic and Security Review Commission, June 9, 2010.

Alan W. Wolff, "The Direction of China's Trade and Industrial Policies," written testimony, hearing on China's Trade Policies, House Ways and Means Committee, June 16, 2010.

The CHAIRMAN. Thank you very much, Dr. Tyson.
Ambassador Hills.

STATEMENT OF HON. CARLA A. HILLS, FORMER U.S. TRADE REPRESENTATIVE, CHAIRPERSON, NATIONAL COMMITTEE ON U.S.-CHINA RELATIONS, WASHINGTON, DC

Ambassador HILLS. First of all, thank you very much, Mr. Chairman, Senator Lugar, and the other members of the committee. It's a great pleasure to appear again before the Senate Foreign Relations Committee.

I think your focus on the economic issues is absolutely indispensable today. I have submitted testimony that responded to your seven questions, and I just picked out three issues that I thought I would summarize, since I was told 5 minutes was the limit. One is trade, one is the imbalance, and, last, the Strategic and Economic Dialogue. And I look forward to your questions.

Our Secretary of State has stated, not once but several times, that our relationship with China is the most important bilateral relationship in the world in this century. And in the area of trade, I would say that is already evident.

Between 2000, the year before China entered the World Trade Organization, and 2008, just before the great recession, United States sales to China increased 340 percent; whereas, during that same period, our sales to the rest of the world increased just 29 percent. And, significantly, every State in the Union has seen near triple-digit growth of their sales to China. Even more significantly, in my opinion, last year, when global trade plummeted 11 percent, pulling global growth into negative territory, our exports to China held steady, where our exports to the rest of the world fell by 20 percent.

And, as Senator Lugar has pointed out, today China is our fastest growing export market, and has become our second-largest export market, behind Canada. And we both benefit from keeping our respective markets open and avoiding all forms of protection, such as Buy America legislation and Buy China policies.

And it is in our mutual interest to work further to open global markets. As Dr. Gary Hufbauer, of the Peterson Institute for International Economics, has calculated, the United States economy is $1 trillion richer per year as a result of our leadership in opening global markets since World War II, and, similarly, it's thanks to open markets that China has achieved double-digit growth for the past three decades that has lifted hundreds of millions of people out of dire poverty.

So, going forward, we should boost our global trade and with it our respective nations' growth by reaching agreement in the Doha Round, and we're more likely to achieve an agreement in those negotiations if the United States and China work together.

In addition, while both of our economies are recovering from the great recession, neither government can ignore the fact that the existing global imbalance risks triggering another serious financial crisis. Indeed, the former chairman of the New York Fed has stated that, even without the housing crisis here in the United States, the global imbalance would have eventually led to the crisis that we have suffered.

Now, China, Germany, Japan, South Korea, and others, have built their growth on exports, accumulating substantial surplus, whereas the United States, the United Kingdom, and Spain, and others, have built their growth on consumption, accumulating substantial debt. Neither growth model is sustainable. And although the United States has cut its external Federal debt from its 6-percent peak in 2006 to about 3 percent last year, it still remains the world's largest debtor nation. And although China has cut its current account surplus from its 11-percent peak in 2007 to about 5 percent in 2009, it still remains the world's largest creditor nation.

And most thoughtful economists suggest that these declines, while welcome, are driven more by cyclical factors than by structural factors. And it's the structural factors that both nations and their colleagues that find themselves in similar circumstance need desperately to address.

To ensure that we do not suffer again from a financial crisis, the global economy simply must be brought into better balance. And this is a global problem. But, if the largest debtor nation and the largest creditor nation were to lead by example and commit to specific structural reforms within realistic timeframes, with periodic updates, that would not only give confidence—great confidence, in my view—to the global market, it would also put our respective economies on a sustainable growth path and ensure the future prosperity of our respective populations.

For example, the United States could commit to a plan at a G20 meeting—we're having a G20 meeting in a couple of days—to bring its primary budget deficit into balance within say 5 years, and its external deficit into better balance in say 10 years, setting forth benchmarks to measure its progress, which it would report at future G20 meetings.

Similarly, China could commit to a plan at a G20 meeting to stimulate its domestic consumption by gradually correcting the underpricing of capital, water, land, and energy that favors its state-owned enterprises and heavy industry, that export, and permitting interest rates to rise on bank deposits, making credit more available to small- and medium-size enterprises, and further loosening the controls over its currency, and providing progress reports in these areas in future G20 meetings.

And the Strategic and Economic Dialogue that was referred to in your questions provides, in my view, an extremely valuable forum for thinking through the tough issues, like rebalancing and protectionism. It brings together Cabinet-level officials on both sides to discuss difficult challenges facing both nations, like the need for further opening the global markets, stimulating innovation, addressing environmental issues, and resolving bilateral differences over trade and investment. Its value could be enhanced by smaller delegations: The last delegation coming from the United States numbered 200, and there was an equal number on the Chinese side; it's tough to achieve a real personal relationship in a group of 400. And more frequent meetings would facilitate the building of the personal relationships, which I deem to be extraordinarily important and key to building mutual trust.

There's so much more that I could say, but I notice the clock is blinking. And so, let me stop. And I am pleased to take your questions.

[The prepared statement of Ambassador Hills follows:]

PREPARED STATEMENT OF HON. CARLA A. HILLS, CHAIR AND CEO OF HILLS & COMPANY, INTERNATIONAL CONSULTANTS, WASHINGTON, DC

Mr. Chairman and members of the committee, thank you for inviting me to share with you my views regarding opportunities and challenges in the United States-China Economic Relationship. You have posed seven questions.

I. WHAT ARE THE KEY ISSUES FOR THE UNITED STATES AND CHINA POLICYMAKERS TO CONSIDER REGARDING FAIR AND OPEN ACCESS TO EACH OTHER'S MARKET?

1. Keeping Bilateral and Global Markets Open

The most important issue for leaders in the United States and in China to keep firmly in mind is that their nation's prosperity requires keeping bilateral and global markets open. History shows that no country has done well by sealing itself off from the world.

Economist Dr. Gary Hufbauer in a comprehensive study published by the Peterson Institute for International Economics calculates that the opening of global markets since World War II has increased our nation's GDP by roughly $1 trillion per year, thus raising the average American household yearly income by $9,500. He further calculates that the additional opening of world markets to trade and investment could increase U.S. wealth potentially by another $500 billion per year, making the average American household richer by an added $4,500 per year. It is hard to think of another economic policy decision that could have such a positive impact on U.S. economic well-being.

And it is thanks to the opening of global markets that China has averaged double digit growth over the past three decades, enabling it to lift hundreds of millions of people out of dire poverty. Today, China has become the world's fastest growing major economy. This year it is likely to replace Japan as the world's second-largest economy.

The benefits of open markets are enormous. The prosperity of the peoples of both China and the United States will be enhanced by maintaining a strong and vibrant economic relationship.

Yet economic hardship inevitably stokes economic nationalism. Last year for the first time since World War II, global trade plummeted 11 percent and global output fell into negative territory. Americans were hit by historic job losses, home foreclosures, and bankruptcies. China did not escape the crisis. It was forced to shutter hundreds of assembly and manufacturing facilities putting millions of people out of work.

Although the International Monetary Fund forecasts world output will grow by more than 4 percent this year and global trade will increase by 7 percent, there is considerable pain remaining. Policymakers in the United States and in China will expedite the economic recovery that is now underway by resisting calls to impose market barriers on the trade or investment of the other.

In spite of our different histories, form of governments, and domestic sensitivities, an important fact for both Chinese and American policymakers to keep in mind is the enormous potential for extremely positive interaction between the largest and the fastest growing economies.

2. Rebalancing Our Economies

While both of our economies are recovering, our policymakers cannot ignore the fact that the imbalance that exists in our respective economies could trigger another crisis. In the last half decade China has become the world's largest creditor nation, and the United States its largest debtor nation. Although China has cut its surplus from its peak in 2007 of 11 percent of its GDP to about 5 percent in 2009 and 3.5 percent in the first quarter of 2010, and the United States external federal deficit has come down about from its peak in 2006 of 6 percent of GDP to 2.8 percent in 2009, thoughtful economists who have studied this issue believe that both declines were largely driven by cyclical factors and that structural changes are still required if we are to protect against future global financial crises.

The United States will need to reduce both its primary budget deficit and its external deficit. China will need to reduce its reliance on exports and heavy industry. Although the action that each government takes to restructure its economy is independent of the other, it is an issue that both policymakers must address.

II. WHAT POTENTIAL DOES THE CHINESE MARKET HOLD FOR U.S. COMPANIES?

The actual and potential of the Chinese market is substantial and growing. China has become America's third-largest export market behind Canada and Mexico and is our fastest growing export market. Between 2000, the year before China joined the World Trade Organization (WTO) and 2008, U.S. sales to China increased 340 percent whereas U.S. sales over that same period to the rest of the world increased just 29 percent.

Importantly, virtually every state in the union has seen near triple digit increases in its sales to China. Last year computers and electronics, crop production, chemicals and transportation equipment comprised our top four exports to China. These are all sectors that generate good domestic jobs.

And in 2009 when for the first time since WWII trade plummeted 11 percent dragging world growth into negative territory, U.S. exports to China held steady whereas U.S. exports to the rest of the world fell nearly 20 percent. This year through April, U.S. exports to China are up 42 percent and are 17 percent higher than the comparable period in 2008.

It is not surprising that U.S. companies continue to seek to do business in and with China. In 2009 in spite of the economic crisis that adversely affected both China and the United States, the value of U.S. goods exported to China was about $70 billion roughly the same amount as before the crisis, and if sales of U.S. goods to Hong Kong are added, the total climbs past $90 billion. In addition, U.S. exports of services to China topped $15 billion. And sales of U.S. affiliates in China topped $84 billion in 2007 before the crisis and the latest year for these statistics. In short, the U.S. current market in China exceeds $100 billion and that market is steadily growing.

III. WHAT ARE THE CHIEF OBSTACLES THAT U.S. COMPANIES FACE IN CHINA?

Foreign companies face a number of obstacles in doing business in China. There are voices in the Chinese leadership, as there are here in the United States and elsewhere, urging the adoption of restrictive measures to protect specific interests of domestic businesses. Measures in China that have been particularly nettlesome to U.S. companies include:

1. Government Procurement: "Indigenous Innovation" Policy

In 2006, China, in an effort to produce "national champions," adopted an "Indigenous Innovation" policy that sought to encourage government purchases of domestic products in specific sectors. Last year the government produced lists of favored products. As a result of bilateral dialogues, the government has moved from mandating domestic purchases to encouraging them. However this "buy China" policy is a major concern to U.S. entrepreneurs, particularly those in the high technology sectors.

2. Protection of Intellectual Property

According to a survey conducted by the United States-China Business Council, two-thirds of U.S. companies found China's failure to protect adequately intellectual property adversely affected their businesses in China. Getting the legal structure right is important. In 2009, the United States brought and won a case in the WTO dealing with copyright infringement which resulted in China amending its laws. However, enforcement is a major problem at the central, provincial and local levels.

3. Standards and Testing

U.S. companies are adversely impacted by standards that are drafted to favor Chinese domestic products. For example, an ingredient that is harmless may be prohibited in a particular product when that ingredient is not used in competing Chinese products.

U.S. companies find China's testing process challenging. A Chinese certification board is responsible for testing most products sold in China. That top-down approach is different from the process used in the United States where industry develops the product standards in the first instance.

4. Investment Restrictions

A United States-China Business Council survey of its member companies doing business in China indicates that roughly 90 percent of its member companies invest in China to reach the market there, not to export back to the United States. Although some sectors are open, others including chemicals, automobiles, telecommunications and express delivery encounter some restrictions. China is in the process of revising its 2007 Catalogue Guiding Foreign Investment in Industry.

IV. HOW CAN THE UNITED STATES BEST STRENGTHEN ITS TRADE AND INVESTMENT TIES WHILE ENSURING U.S. COMPETITIVENESS IN AN INCREASINGLY COMPETITIVE ENVIRONMENT?

Our Nation can strengthen its trade and investment ties with the trading nations of the world including China in a number of ways including (1) leading the 153 members of the World Trade Organization (WTO) to a successful conclusion of the Doha Round of Multilateral Negotiations; (2) expanding efforts to open markets with the 21 economies comprising the Asia Pacific Economic Cooperation forum (APEC) starting with completing the Trans-Pacific Partnership; (3) approving the three pending free trade agreements that have been signed with South Korea, Colombia, and Panama; (4) completing the negotiation of a Bilateral Investment Treaty with China; and (5) addressing our restrictions on immigration that reduce our competitiveness.

1. Doha

For six decades the United States under both Democratic and Republican administrations led the world in opening global markets to trade and investment with the result that economic growth both globally and nationally soared for rich and poor nations alike. Our actions in the early multilateral negotiations under the General Agreement on Tariffs and Trade (GATT) accelerated the economic rebuilding of nations devastated by World War II. Today we could be equally far sighted by achieving an agreement in the Doha Round of Multilateral Negotiations that would integrate developing nations more solidly into the global trade regime and in so doing enlarge trade and investment opportunities that would fuel economic growth at home and around the world. Unfortunately, we are no longer leading efforts to open global markets.

Currently in its ranking of 133 trading nations, the World Economic Forum ranks the United States behind 43 nations in terms of how open the domestic market is to trade. However, the Doha Round offers our Nation an outstanding opportunity to do well by doing good. One example stands out. By agreeing to reduce meaningfully our agricultural subsidies, we could persuade other governments with high subsidies to do the same. Opening global agricultural markets would not only benefit our farm exporters, but it would show the world that we are serious about taking steps to put our Nation on more a more sustainable fiscal path.

2. APEC and TPP

Expanding our trade and investment ties in Asia offers the United States a significant opportunity to stimulate domestic economic growth and job creation. The 21 members of the Asia Pacific Economic Cooperation forum (APEC) represent approximately 2.5 billion consumers, 58 percent of global trade, and more than half of world output. Over the past decade most of the increase in global growth has been generated by the APEC economies. Collectively these economies account for a majority of our Nation's exports. Further opening these markets to U.S. entrepreneurs would enhance our Nation's competitiveness in the world's most vibrant region where other major trading nations including China, Japan, South Korea, the European Union and the economies comprising the Association of Southeast Asian Nations (ASEAN) have negotiated or are currently negotiating bilateral and plurilateral trade agreements that advantage their entrepreneurs over ours. Obtaining equal or better access to these markets would enhance our Nation's competitiveness, create jobs, and boost growth.

Achieving this will require leadership and action on our part. To strengthen our trade and investment ties in this high-growth region, we should move forward promptly to negotiate the Trans-Pacific Partnership (TPP),[1] which could serve as a first step toward a broad market opening agreement in the region which over time could incorporate additional APEC members, such as Japan, South Korea, Indonesia, Malaysia, and eventually China. Such an agreement would not only enhance our Nation's competitive position, it would also create a visible bond across the Pacific to work against the world splintering into three blocs (Asia, Europe, and the Americas) which would both impede global and national economic growth and increase the potential for global instability. The APEC summit in Hawaii in 2011 gives the United States an excellent opportunity to showcase a completed TPP, which would demonstrate its renewed commitment to the region.

3. Approval of Pending Free Trade Agreements

A. Korea Free Trade Agreement

Approval of the Korean Free Trade Agreement would both enhance our competitiveness in Asia and demonstrate our continued interest in the region. Under its terms South Korea, currently our seventh-largest trading partner, would open its market to U.S. farm products, goods, and services, enhance its protection of intellectual property and substantially open government procurement. Ninety-five percent of bilateral trade in consumer and industrial products would become duty free within 3 years. The agreement would cause trade to expand between our two nations and stimulate both economic growth and jobs in both markets and put our entrepreneurs on an equal footing with the growing list of major trading nations that have already negotiated trade agreements with South Korea.[2] Significantly, it has indicated an interest in negotiating a trade agreement with China, which if concluded, would put our exporters at a substantial disadvantage in one of our key export markets.

B. Colombia and Panama Free Trade Agreements

Approval of the trade agreements that the United States has signed but not ratified with Colombia and Panama would substantially enhance our competitiveness in Latin America. Colombia with its $250 billion economy is the second-largest in South America. Today in excess of 90 percent of U.S. imports from Colombia enter the United States duty free while relatively high tariffs are imposed on most U.S. exports. The agreement would eliminate 80 percent of those tariffs and open up markets to a broad range of services and investment. That would make exports more competitive and remove the additional disadvantage our exporters face not only by "leveling the playing field" between the two countries but also by achieving equality with Colombia's other trading partners like Canada that have already entered a free trade agreement with Colombia.

Similarly opening Panama's market would make our goods, services, and investment more competitive. It makes no sense for us to be the impediment that enables Panama to ship its products duty free and to assess duties on our services and goods including our competitive heavy equipment used for canal upgrades when much of our competition ships duty free.

4. Bilateral Investment Treaty With China

As economist Dr. Hufbauer has ably documented U.S. outward foreign investment pulls U.S. exports into the foreign market, while inward foreign investment into the United States boosts economic growth and creates domestic jobs. To establish clear rules governing inward investment gives certainty to the market and confidence to

---

[1] Currently involving Australia, Brunei, Chile, New Zealand, Peru, Singapore, the United States and Vietnam.

[2] Korea currently has five free trade agreements in effect, two that are signed and pending ratification, negotiations underway with eight other countries and is considering entering negotiations with six more.

investors, plus it helps to avoid controversy. In June 2008 at the fourth Strategic Economic Dialogue, China and the United States agreed to begin negotiations of a bilateral investment treaty to protect the interests of their respective investors in the other's economy. Such an agreement would protect our investors against discriminatory measures that today account for a major portion of the obstacles that confront our businesses in China. With economic nationalism on the rise in both countries, moving ahead to conclude an investment treaty would enhance U.S. competitiveness by insuring that we can capture the growth and jobs that attend cross border investment.

5. Immigration Contributes to U.S. Competitiveness

We usually talk of trade ties in terms of goods, services, and investment and less frequently mention people and ideas. Yet the United States is a nation of immigrants. Talented people from all over the world come to work or study in the United States bringing their ideas, starting businesses, creating jobs and contributing to our competitiveness. According to a study published in 2008 by the Small Business Administration,[3] immigrants constitute 12.5 percent of U.S. businessowners and start 25 percent of new engineering and technology companies. Another study published in 2009 by the American Electronics Association,[4] found that immigrants were CEOs or lead technologists in one of four technology and engineering companies started in the United States between 1995 and 2005. These immigrant-founded companies employed 450,000 workers and generated $52 billion in revenues in 2006. Unfortunately for our economic growth, creation of new jobs, and overall competitiveness the annual number of H–1B visas is sharply restricted. Current law limits H–1B visas to 65,000 annually with up to 20,000 available for foreign nationals holding advanced degrees from an American university. America could boost its growth, job creation, and competitiveness by opening its doors more widely to talent from beyond its border.

V. THE STRATEGIC AND ECONOMIC DIALOGUE IS OUR BILATERAL FORUM FOR ENGAGEMENT ON MANY OF THESE ISSUES. HOW WOULD YOU RATE THE EFFECTIVENESS ON THESE ISSUES?

I believe that the Strategic and Economic Dialogue is an important bilateral forum that can help our government to build a solid relationship with the world's fastest growing economy. It provides the opportunity for our leaders at the highest level to meet their counterparts and discuss critical issues. These discussions can enhance our understanding of China's economic challenges as well as its strategic objectives and ensure that China's leaders understand ours. Mutual understanding is indispensable to finding solutions to tough issues. The list of economic issues that require collaboration for proper resolution is long and growing including rebalancing our national and the global economies, energy security, trade policy, financial reform, and environmental protection. To address effectively these and other issues, it is overwhelmingly in our national interest to maintain a close, candid, and collaborative relationship at the highest levels, and the Strategic and Economic Dialogues help to do just that.

We know that high-level engagement works. In recent years our Deputy Secretary of State met frequently to discuss issues of foreign policy. In addition our Secretary of the Treasury led the effort called the Strategic Economic Dialogue (SED) whereby Cabinet-level officials from both governments met to discuss economic issues for 2 days twice a year. The purpose of the SED was to discuss complex, longstanding, economic challenges and to craft solutions satisfactory to both governments.

Since both our governments are quite compartmentalized and have different organizational structures, these meetings helped to circumvent the stovepipe structures that impede decisions by bringing to the table all the high-level officials on both sides required for a decision.

These face-to-face meetings enabled both sides to understand the concerns of their counterparts and led to a number of positive outcomes. For example in 2007 when food and safety issues were very much in the news, high-level officials from both governments seriously discussed at an SED meeting effective ways to deal with these issues.

At the next meeting of the SED, representatives of our Food and Drug Administration and our Consumer Products Safety Commission and their Chinese counter-

---

[3] Robert W. Fairlie "Estimating the Contribution of Immigrant Business Owners to the U.S. Economy," Small Business Administration Office of Advocacy, November 2008, http://www.sha.gov/advo/research/rs334tot.pdf.

[4] "Workforce & Immigration Overview: Maintaining a High-Skilled U.S. Technology Workforce," 2009, http://www.acanet.org/GovernmentAffairs/gaet_1B_HIBVisa.asp.

parts were able to announce a Memorandum of Understanding covering how they would cooperate in food and safety investigations. Representatives of our FDA have publicly stated that they had never before enjoyed such a high level of positive interaction with their counterparts in China. They have established offices in Beijing, Guangzhou, and Shanghai.

More recently at the S&ED meeting this past May, after discussion the Chinese Government agreed to submit a proposal to join the WTO Government Procurement Agreement by the end of July. Such an agreement would protect our entrepreneurs against some of the discrimination that they name as the top obstacle they encounter today in penetrating the Chinese market.

The economic dialogues not only provided an effective forum for raising and solving economic issues of concern to both our governments, but they also created a mechanism that avoids having to initiate talks among strangers in the heat of a crisis.

Accordingly I was very pleased when it was announced that our Secretaries of State and Treasury would share leadership of a high-level bilateral dialogue, now called the Strategic and Economic Dialogue. The S&ED first met in July last year and again last month for 2 days on each occasion. The plan is to hold these meetings on an annual basis dedicating one day to a plenary session and the second day to separate discussions on economic and strategic issues.

The one downside that I see in the new structure is its sheer size. In May our delegation to Beijing comprised 200 senior officials, the largest U.S. delegation to China in the history of our bilateral relationship. The merged strategic and the economic groups bring together such a large number of participants that relationship-building that has been so helpful in the past will be far more difficult.

Another downside I see is that the stated intention is to meet yearly rather than twice each year. Formerly, two full days twice a year, four days total, were devoted to economic discussions. Now only one day each year will be devoted exclusively to economic issues. Our bilateral economic agenda is long and growing longer which suggests to me the need for more rather than fewer meetings.

There are two other bilateral dialogues that provide valuable means to have sustained focus on critical economic issues, but they are not conducted at the same high level. One is the Joint Commission on Commerce and Trade, a senior officials group that has formed some 17 working groups to address specific issues including industrial and competition policy, intellectual property, information technology, and trade and industry. Most of these plan to meet twice a year.

The second is the United States-China Investment Forum, a deputies led group that is focused on such issues as procurement, standards, and access to markets for services.

VI. CAN WE MAXIMIZE OUR ABILITY TO ADDRESS CONCERNS ABOUT CERTAIN CHINESE ECONOMIC POLICIES THROUGH MULTILATERAL FORA SUCH AS THE G20?

The G20 group of nations representing the world's 20 largest economies which has replaced the G8 representing the eight large industrialized nations is far better equipped to deal with today's global economic challenges.

Three issues of key importance to both the United States and China are better suited to the G20 forum than bilateral discussion: (1) China's currency regime; (2) the need to rebalance the global economy; and (3) the need to keep global markets open in the face of domestic calls for protectionism.

1. China's Currency Regime

China's currency controls have been an issue of contention not only with the United States, but also with the European Union, which is China's largest trading partner, as well as a number of other nations. China's announcement a few days ago that it will permit the yuan to gradually appreciate will help to reduce those tensions. Monitoring this issue at future G20 meetings will be helpful in that it will maximize pressure on China which wants to be seen as constructive in international fora and minimizes bilateral contention.

2. Rebalancing the Global Economy

The global recovery that is currently underway, faster for some than for others, could be derailed by the serious imbalance of the global economy that has ballooned in recent years. China, Germany, Japan, South Korea, and other Asian economies have built their growth on exports, whereas the United States, the United Kingdom, and Spain among others have relied excessively on domestic consumption, particularly in the housing sector, to fuel economic growth.

Although investment excesses by the financial sector triggered the fiscal crisis in 2008, there is general agreement that the global imbalance made the crisis much worse. As stated last year by Gerald Corrigan, former President of the New York Federal Reserve: "It is highly likely that these imbalances would create a serious macroeconomic problem even if we had not had the fiscal problem."

If we are to protect against future global financial crises, the global economy must be brought into better balance. That will require debtor and creditor nations to alter their existing economic models to put their economies on a more sustainable growth plan. Debtor nations cannot continue to consume at the excessive levels of the past, and creditor nations must look more to their own consumers to fuel their economic growth.

This is a global problem and requires a global solution. However, global balance is more likely to be restored if the world's largest debtor nation and its largest creditor nation were to lead by example with each committing to specific structural reforms, spelling out the steps that each would take within specific timeframes, and agreeing to provide periodic updates regarding progress. That would boost confidence in the future health and stability of the global market, which in turn would help keep our respective domestic economies on a sustainable growth path.

The required changes will take time to implement. But a plan of action over a period of years could be announced that would give confidence to the market and to investors. One could imagine the United States announcing a plan at a G20 meeting to bring its primary budget deficit into balance within a specified period like 5 years and its external deficit into balance in a specified period like 10 years and to report regularly at future G20 meetings on its progress.

Similarly, one could imagine China announcing at a G20 meeting a plan to stimulate its domestic consumption by correcting its underpricing of capital, water, land, and energy to large enterprises, permitting interest rates to rise on bank deposits, making credit more available to small- and medium-size businesses, and continuing the steady and gradual loosening of controls on the yuan that it announced this past weekend with progress reports on these structural changes at future G20 meetings.

Such a commitment by the United States to undertake structural reform necessary to achieve more balanced growth would not be a favor granted to nor conditioned on action by China, nor would a decision by China to make structural changes to stimulate domestic consumption be a favor granted to or conditioned on action by the United States.

The policy corrections that each needs to make are necessary to ensure each nation's future financial stability and prosperity, for if corrections are not made the global imbalance will likely ignite another economic crisis. By their respective actions, they would not only give confidence to the market but also help persuade other nations with imbalances to follow their lead. The G20 provides an appropriate forum.

3. Keeping Global Markets Open

Leaders of the G20 nations which account for 85 percent of world output and 80 percent of world trade have taken a leadership role with respect to the global economy. They meet biannually to consult and collaborate on critical global economic issues.

The G20 leaders instead of simply pledging support could take action and make history by bringing the Doha Round to a successful conclusion. Economic studies document that the reductions in trade barriers that could be secured in this round of trade talks would boost world output between $300 billion and $700 billion a year. We need that growth now.

VII. WHAT ARE YOUR BROAD VIEWS ON THE IMPORTANCE OF THE ECONOMIC RELATIONSHIP AS PART OF A LARGER FOREIGN POLICY AGENDA?

There is no question but that a collaborative, constructive economic relationship creates a positive environment for discussing tough and contentious foreign policy issues. Even where national interests on foreign challenges diverge, a solid economic relationship makes serious discussion of and possible narrowing of those differences more likely.

That does not mean that we should forgo pressing our economic interests. From time to time we will have economic differences with our large and important trading partners, including China. When we believe that China or any trading partner has violated recognized rules of the WTO, or the rules of other international agreements, we should act and use the dispute settlement mechanisms provided to resolve the problem. And where the rules of the system are insufficient, we should negotiate to ensure that they reflect market realities.

Our government has taken China to the WTO eight times. We have settled four of the cases, won three and have one pending. China has brought five cases against us. We have settled one, won two, and lost two.

This is how the WTO trade regime should work. It enables us to resolve trade issues under mutually agreed transparent rules minimizing friction.

CONCLUSION

Managing United States-China relations presents challenges but also very substantial opportunities. Many in America ask: Can the world's largest and fastest growing economies constructively work together to enhance our future prosperity and stability? Or have the differences between our increasingly competitive economies along with those differences in our histories, forms of government, and domestic sensitivities become too great to enable us to harness our respective strengths to deal effectively with today's bilateral and global challenges?

My answer is that we can, should, and must work constructively together. Most importantly, I believe that by doing so we can build habits of cooperation that will help us deal effectively with new challenges as they arise which will not only enhance the well-being of the people of the United States and of China but will contribute meaningfully to global peace and stability.

The CHAIRMAN. Well, Ambassador Hills, Dr. Tyson, thank you very much. You've put a lot of food for thought on the table, and I want to pick up in a few places right away.

Ambassador, you just mentioned that China's open markets have resulted in the double-digit growth. A lot of people would argue about how open that market really is; sort of a one-way street, in some people's opinion.

I was over there recently, meeting with a bunch of our companies, all of whom complained about the Chinese Government bidding process and procurement process, and how really impossible it was for them. You know, they'd bid, they'd do well, but they never got chosen. It was always a domestic company or a majority-owned company. It's always, you know, China-centric.

Now, that works very effectively for them, obviously. And with the kind of growth that they've had and the opportunities they've had, a lot of people are willing to, you know, put their money down and go for it.

But, it's not creating the kind of—I mean, the single biggest effect on this question of the current accounts deficit—on our current accounts deficit while we've gone up the 300 percent as you've mentioned, it's nowhere near where it ought to be, nor is their consumption commitment where it ought to be.

So, I mean given the clear penchant for the Chinese to kind of do what they want, when they want, which is what they've done on the renminbi, the reevaluation—way late, not enough, in some people's view—so, it's sort of an incremental deal, which won't have the kind of impact it ought to.

So, help us understand, if you would, is there any leverage? Do you have any leverage with your banker—your biggest banker? Do we have any ability to do anything except ask and hope?

Ambassador HILLS. Well, first of all——

The CHAIRMAN. It's not a new topic. We've been going through this through several administrations, and it's not getting better, it's getting worse.

Ambassador HILLS. Mr. Chairman, I would say that our trade with China over the last decade has soared. The figures that I gave you, of a 340-percent increase and China becoming this year our second-largest export market, is really remarkable for a country that, in 1978, was a Communist country, sealed off from the rest of the world. It's remarkable progress in three decades.

And if you look at where our trade deficit has gone, in 1998 the composition of our trade deficit—it was 75 percent in East Asia; today, it is 49 percent in East Asia and 51 percent with the rest of the world. And when I say "East Asia," of course, I include China.

The CHAIRMAN. Can I just ask you a question, interspersed there? Is that because you're sort of heralding the upside? You can look at it and see the glass, you know, in different ways, here. But, is the upside of that because China has so successfully brought so many people in from the agricultural sector, into an urbanized and production role, that they're able—that it sort of suits their interests, it's in their interest to have the particular products come in that come in, but they're still highly selective about what that is, and how much? Even though it's gone up significantly, we're still at an enormous deficit, in terms of our overall debt relationship, and way behind where we could be, in terms of boosting our own economy and kicking the entire global economy into gear.

Ambassador HILLS. Mr. Chairman, I was trying to answer the question you posed regarding the degree of openness in the China market. And the fact that our deficit with East Asia has declined with China being part of it suggests that it's been opened. It also accounts for the amount of trade that China has invited in.

One of the reasons why our deficit has shifted from East Asia being so large a part, down, is because China has invited in Japan, Taiwan, Singapore, South Korea, and they are producing products in China. Many of the products produced in China are made in China, but not by China. When you buy an iPod, it comes to our shore at a cost of about $150, and $4 of that value is Chinese, which is based upon snapping together component parts from Japan, South Korea, and the United States.

But having said that, the Chinese market is quite open by Asian standards. They're not as open as the United States. Their average tariff is about 9 percent, versus ours, at about 3. And we want to continue to work with them to open their market. They're far more open than India, they're far more open than Indonesia, but they're not as open as the United States, which has been working on this since World War II.

And you're absolutely right; there are some very tough restrictions. I listed them in my testimony. Industrial policies and restrictions in the form of threatened compulsory licensing, preferences for domestic products, subsidies for domestic production are real problems. We lump these restrictions together as "Indigenous Innovation." These policies are of growing concern to our companies. Our Buy America is an irritant to the Chinese. We have issues that we should sit down and talk about. And I think that, when we do, it does help to make progress.

And we also have the G20, which, as Laura Tyson has suggested, is a good forum when others share our concern. For example, on the revaluing of the currency, Europe, as well as we, believes that the currency is undervalued, to the detriment of their exports. By having a wider group of nations object to or encourage change in certain of China's restrictive policies, is helpful, for China wants to be on the international stage, and it wants to be respected. And so, it has made a number of changes, which are very much in its own interest, for example, to control inflation and to increase consumption through expenditures on social programs.

The CHAIRMAN. Well, let me ask you both, quickly, if I can—my time's up, but I wanted to get this question on the table, quickly. And, Dr. Tyson, maybe you begin.

To what degree is this economic surge by China activating, in your judgment—we've had a lot of focus on the economic side of this—a more assertive foreign policy, perhaps the rapid military modernization, and to what end, and mercantilist economic policy, to some degree?

Dr. Tyson.

Dr. TYSON. OK. I don't really feel that I'm an expert on their military policy. And I do think that, in areas that are trade-related and economic-related—and that can include aid policies to the rest of the world, the organization structure of multilateral institutions, and right down to a particular bilateral trade dispute on indigenous innovation, the Chinese are becoming more assertive.

It's not just because they have done so well, but also because, frankly, the U.S. economy has stumbled badly, and, I think, around the world, the recognition that we have stumbled badly leads our trading partners to be more assertive in their relations with us. I think we have to look, therefore, to ourselves, of what we are going to do to restore our own economy on a very strong growth path, sound fiscal policy, going forward.

On the issue—I just will say one thing where I think maybe Ambassador Hills and I have somewhat of a disagreement—I certainly agree, on the import side, looking at our imports from China—it's really important to understand that much of what we import from China we would have imported from other places, and it's moved to China to be put together and sold to us. And the Chinese rightly point out, all the time, that the value of their exports to us, or our imports from them on average, 25 percent of that value is Chinese-value-added, it's stuff they've imported. And if we were to slap significant tariffs on those products, the production would shift gradually out of China, but it wouldn't come back here. It wouldn't come back here. So, we—I think we have to be very cognizant of what—why that import imbalance looks the way it is.

On the export side, however, I think the Chinese are moving in ways which I think deserve our attention. They are committed to becoming a technologically innovative nation. They want to move from a labor-intensive, low-value-added industry structure to a high-value-added technology structure. And that's where the indigenous innovation policy comes from, and preferential government procurement, and standards. The Chinese want to develop their own standard for things where there are global standards already that are perfectly acceptable. And when you sort of look at them doing this, you say, "This looks like it could be in violation of their agreement on standards at the WTO." You're not supposed to create standards for the purpose of affecting trade flows.

So, these are really tough issues, because they're nontariff barriers. And the protections in the WTO either don't exist, in some case, or they're inadequate; it's very hard to bring a case, and win.

I think the United States, therefore, really has to engage the Chinese on these issues directly. And, by the way, I think the concern of the American business community, which I've also picked up, has actually been extremely helpful, because the U.S. Government now is taking a much tougher position on these things. The Chinese for a very long time, were very open to these companies. These major American companies that have become a major part of their economy—are now saying, "We're not being treated appropriately or fairly." That becomes a very powerful, I think, lever for trying to get some negotiating progress on these issues with China.

So, I think they've become more important, and I think we should focus on them at the top of our list of priorities.

The CHAIRMAN. Senator Lugar.

Senator LUGAR. Ambassador Hills, your written testimony notes that, "Immigrant-founded companies employed 450,000 workers and generated $52 billion in revenues in 2006." Now, recently, with Senator Kerry, I introduced the Startup Visa Act of 2010, to allow an immigrant entrepreneur to receive a 2-year visa if he or she can show that a qualified U.S. investor is willing to dedicate a significant sum, a minimum of $250,000, for the immigrant's startup venture.

What do you expect the impact of such legislation to be? Is it at the right levels? And, second, leaving aside the visa aspect, is it likely that Chinese companies will simply make much larger investments now in our economy? I read that, for example, they've noted that, as the labor costs have risen in China, it makes more sense to produce the goods and services in the United States.

On these issues, can you give us some additional comment?

Ambassador HILLS. Let me say that my comment about the immigration and the need to open our nation to bright minds and to the development of new technology is in response to the question of enhancing our competitiveness. The statistics that we have in the Department of Commerce and Small Business Administration document the high number of startups created by foreign-born, the substantial amount of jobs they create, and the substantial amount of growth that they contribute to our economy. So, I support your Start Up Visa Act. I believe that 65,000 H1B Visas for a country of over 300 million people is extraordinarily limited, plus it is very, very difficult and time-consuming to get a H–1B visas for people who want to come to the United States. It's also very difficult for a student to come here to study. A student can be accepted at one of our major universities, and not be permitted to come to the United States, or, after graduating, cannot be permitted to stay. We're just cutting ourselves off from talent and new ideas.

I was in China last week, and I addressed the issue of indigenous innovation, and I said, "You're hurting yourself by turning inward. When you keep out an idea, an invention, a patent, because you prefer to have it made at home, you hurt yourself not only for the loss of the idea or invention but also, because you create a monopoly protected from competition has little incentive to innovate. That protected company is not going to expend money to become more competitive or move up the value chain. But if you were to let all the ideas, inventions, patents come in without government interference; it would stimulate ideas in your domestic market. So, you're hurting yourself."

I think there's a deal here to be made that benefits both sides. In exchange for a relaxation of our export controls, China could set aside those domestic industrial policies often grouped under the name "indigenous innovation." And I truly believe that.

On the investment side, I believe that Chinese companies are thinking more and more of investing abroad. We need to take care that we do not discriminate. And we see, particularly in the south of our country, there are some small investments from the Chinese. But, they express concern, having tried to invest in some larger segments and not fully understanding CFIUS—Committee on Foreign Investment in the United States—that operates pursuant to section 721 of the Defense Production Act of 1950, as amended, and the regulations that we have—that it is difficult to invest here. And they read our press, and they believe that their investors will be discriminated against, that they are not thought well of in our country. I think that's untrue. I think that most Americans think very well of the Chinese, applaud their miraculous rise from dire poverty to where they are today. And, although China's GDP on a per capita basis is only about one-tenth the size of ours while their GDP is roughly one-third of ours, they continue to make rapid progress. Still China has a number of challenges—e.g., environmental, demographic, and growing income disparity—but it is making progress.

Senator LUGAR. So, I gather that your sense is, essentially there are a good number of Chinese who are prepared to come to the United States and make investments—that is, personally locate themselves here—if our visa situation was friendlier. And with regard to investment in the United States, if our investment climate was perceived as more friendly, these investments would come. Therefore, at least some of us might argue that, in terms of creating more American jobs now and having more capital in the country, our diplomacy really needs an uptick so that there is a different set of perceptions.

Ambassador HILLS. I would agree with you entirely. I think we ought to open our market to foreign investment. If someone wants to invest a dollar or an RMB in our market, and create jobs and good products, that's to our benefit.

Senator LUGAR. Let me ask Dr. Tyson this question, that, in your written testimony, you note a significant appreciation of the RMB, relative to the dollar, will not have a significant effect on U.S. trade deficit or on U.S. employment.

Dr. TYSON. Right.

Senator LUGAR. But, what measures, if any, vis-a-vis China, would have a real impact on the trade deficit or the unemployment rate?

Dr. TYSON. So, what I was trying to say in that observation was that, basically, what matters to the overall U.S. trade imbalance is not the relationship with any one country. That was the first point.

The second point is the point that I mentioned earlier. I think a significant—a dramatic overnight appreciation of the renminbi, versus the dollar, would initially raise prices of a significant number of important imports to middle-class Americans, and a lot of it would quickly leave China; it would go to different locations. It wouldn't change our trade imbalance.

So, I tend to see our trade imbalance as not very sensitive to an appreciation. Now, I know that Fred Bergsten's numbers are if you had an appreciation, I think, of 20 percent over a 5-year period, you'd get a million U.S. jobs and a reduction of the U.S. trade deficit of $150 billion. The problem with that statement is that we had something like a 20-percent appreciation of the RMB between 2005 and 2008, and this was the period when the U.S. trade deficit was going through the roof, and when the U.S. current account imbalance hit a peak as a share of GDP.

So, I think the link between that currency value and the U.S. trade imbalance is a very weak link, and I would prefer us to think about the other factors that influence that.

I just want to add, because I completely agree, and you saw me nodding my head, about the importance of inviting, or certainly not in any way deterring, Chinese investment in the United States. The Chinese have a massive amount—the largest holdings of United States-dollar assets in the world—and they are looking for ways to diversify those assets. They are worried about what the value of those assets will be as the renminbi does climb, relative to the dollar. They're worried about what happens to those assets if we get a spike in U.S. interest rates. They're worried about inflation in the United States over the next 20 years. They would like to diversify those assets.

They don't have a lot of options. The Euro has kind of disappeared as an option, so they're not going to, I think, buy a lot of gold and, you know, put it in a building.

I think they would like to diversify into other U.S. assets. And we are either the first or the second—depending upon, I suppose, the month—largest destination for foreign direct investment in the world. China's the other one. We welcome foreign direct investment from the rest of the world. We need to be sure we welcome it from China, because it is a better way, frankly, to alleviate our trade imbalance with China because some of the stuff we buy from China, imported, we will buy here.

And if you think about the history of the United States trade imbalance with Japan, when we had significant friction with them in certain sectors, the Japanese moved production facilities here. And today, they produce significant amounts of product, with significant amounts of American-employed labor, using their technology, here.

So, yes, I think this is very important.

Senator LUGAR. Well, I thank you very much. I would just underline the thought that we really ought to be thinking in terms of how we suggest to the Chinese they invest in our country——

Dr. TYSON. Yes.

Senator LUGAR [continuing]. In addition to simply loaning us money.

Dr. TYSON. Yes.

Senator LUGAR. It's a very different——

Dr. TYSON. Exactly.

Senator LUGAR [continuing]. Concept, in terms of our own employment and our own economic growth.

Dr. TYSON. Yes.

Senator LUGAR. And I appreciate both of your answers.

Thank you.

The CHAIRMAN. Thanks, Senator Lugar.

Senator Casey.

Senator CASEY. Dr. Tyson, thank you.

Dr. TYSON. Thank you.

Senator CASEY. Ambassador Hills, thank you so much for your testimony.

I wanted to put my first question in the context of our current economic climate. When I speak of Pennsylvania, I think it's emblematic of a lot of places. We are, in our State, at about 9.1 percent unemployment, but that's 591,000 people, at last count—almost 600,000—a big, big number. And although I think we are in a recovery, we've got a long way to go.

One of the persistent, nagging, and most difficult challenges we face is the problem of trade deficits. And we've got States like Pennsylvania that are heavily exposed to, or impacted by, the trade imbalance between the United States and China. There's obviously been a manufacturing component to that.

But, I guess recently the Alliance for American Manufacturing reported that, contrary to some of the conventional wisdom, it's not simply, or only, manufacturing jobs, but high-technology jobs, as well, that industry.

Another study, by the Economic Policy Institute, over a 7-year period, in terms of what happened in Pennsylvania, a net job loss of more than 95,000, due to the trade deficits with China.

So, all of that is predicate to a good deal of what you've already spoken to. I know that, Dr. Tyson, you have a series of recommendations, starting at page 17 of your testimony. And I know that, Ambassador Hills, you've got a series beginning on page 3—a series of obstacles that you set forth as the obstacles that our companies face with regard to China.

Where's the—if you had to—if you bumped into a—on the street, a constituent of mine in Pennsylvania, or a similarly situated State, when they ask you, "How do we bridge that gap, how do we begin to—at least begin to chip away at the problem?"—what are the two or three strategic steps you think we have to take, in the near term, to begin to put in place a strategy to get out of that hole?

And I—either one of you want to take a crack at it, or both?

Ambassador HILLS. When you talk about the imbalance that concerns your constituents, we obviously have to bring, not only our bilateral, but our global imbalance into equilibrium. That's going to take both the United States along with other deficit nations and China along with other surplus nations to alter their models of growth. Those in deficit cannot point their finger at the surplus nation and say, "You are exporting too much." Nor can the surplus nations point their finger at deficit nations and say you are consuming too much." Both groups need to change their growth models. It is true that China needs to stimulate its domestic consumption for its own national interests. It is also true that its currency is somewhat undervalued, and appreciation would help to stimulate domestic consumption. But appreciation of the currency is not a silver bullet. Currency is a factor. But, removing the distortions in the factors of production—land, water, fuel, and finance—are undoubtedly far more important factors in stimulating domestic consumption. China's growth model for the past three decades has been built on growth generated by large state-owned enterprises that export. And even the foreign investors that came in from Japan and East Asia also were primarily manufacturing and assembling goods for export. And those exports go on the account of China with the result that China has the largest trade surplus.

That is not sustainable. This must change. In China it's creating enormous environmental problems and is contributing to a wage gap between rural and urban areas. When you take the five largest of the heavy industry, they are responsible for most of the pollution. Heavy metal pollution destroys about 1,700 square miles of productive farm land each year and contributes to the fact that most of China's urban ground water is polluted. In addition China is home to the most polluted cities in the world. In 2007 the World Bank reported that 16 of the world's most polluted cities are in China. And so, for domestic reasons, China needs to change its model of growth that up to now has been disproportionately based on heavy industry and export. China has many challenges, including demographic challenges that they're going to have to deal with. And with 1.3 billion people, they can and need to stimulate domestic consumption to boost growth. That will help develop small and medium industries and service providers. Moving to a growth model that relies more on consumption will make the Chinese population much more satisfied, and make your constituents much less anxious.

Now, at the same time, I'm sure some anxiety in Pennsylvania is connected to the fact that our deficit—our primary budget deficit—has grown to levels that frighten people, and our accumulated external debt adds to their anxiety. And so, we also must change our growth model. We can no longer rely disproportionately on domestic consumption, both public and private, to fuel our economic growth. We must get control of our fiscal deficit and boost private savings. And whether we adopt a "pay-as-you-go" program, and really mean it, or some other fiscal discipline, we need to get our fiscal house in order. That would provide, I think, substantial assurance at home and abroad that the United States economy was not going to have to go through a great recession in the next decade.

So, there's a lot that both China and the United States have to do.

Senator CASEY. Dr. Tyson.

Dr. TYSON. You've asked a very hard question, because I don't know, for example, the numbers of workers you announced that lost their jobs. I don't know how many would have been to a movement of a production facility to China or an import from China. I do know that.

Let's take what's going on right now. In the last year, we've seen, particularly the last 6 months, quite strong growth in industrial production in the United States. We have seen a quite strong export of manufactured goods in the United States to China and the other emerging market economies. This has been associated with no growth in employment in manufacturing in the United States. That is not, therefore, a trade issue; that is a technology issue. That is how the U.S. companies compete, globally, with building manufacturing products here, and ramping them up, which they're doing right now, without increases in employment, because the technology has displaced the employment.

And one of our issues in the United States is, we have to be clear, when employment numbers like that show up, what is it that's the role of China's development strategy. It may actually be not very important to the employment problem.

Another thing I would say——

Senator CASEY. You mean attribution.

Dr. TYSON. Yes. But, I would find it very difficult to talk to such a person, because, you know, first of all, I would have to understand. I mean, the second thing I would say is—Ambassador Hills mentioned that the Chinese encourage their enterprises through low interest rate through subsidies. They encourage certain things. They want to develop their economy in a certain way so they subsidize certain things.

What did we subsidize in the United States, heavily, that was part of the crisis? Housing. We subsidize. We absolutely subsidize residential construction in the United States. And a number of workers—25 percent, as far as I know, last count—of the unemployed problem in the United States is construction workers, who were very important to the boom that we created with our own interest-rate subsidy policy in the United States.

We don't have subsidy policies to create industrial employment. We don't believe in them. We don't do them. China does them. China absolutely does them. And they've built a very powerful employment base in manufacturing.

So, I think—and then, the last thing I would say—in looking at Pennsylvania's trade imbalance, or any country—or any State trade imbalance—at the end of the day, I'm not sure what it would look like in Pennsylvania, because there is a huge amount of products being bought in Pennsylvania in retail outlets that are primarily bought in China, and there is service employment in the United States that's supported by those imports.

Now, this gets me to another problem in the United States. We have a polarization of the workforce going on. It's very dramatic. The unemployment rate is not high—it's high, but not that high— for people with a college education or higher. It's around 5 to 6 percent right now, in that range. The 15-percent unemployment rates are for high-school, or less-than-high-school, educated workers. And those middle-income manufacturing jobs, that used to be a way through, for those people, to the middle class, don't exist anymore. And I would say, not because of trade with China, but because technology has displaced those jobs.

So, we have a huge educational challenge in the country, because where the jobs are likely to grow in the future over the next 5 years are in college-educated and more. And right now we're making it more difficult, in many respects. In many States the tuitions for college education are going through the roof because of State budget problems.

So, the Chinese, I would say, are restructuring their economy. They're building infrastructure in the center and western regions. They're introducing new social security policies that will reduce the household savings rate in China. They're doing real, structural things that will change their growth strategy over time.

I don't think we're doing those. And I don't think a path to credible deficit reduction, which we need—I'm not saying we don't need it—but, that, by itself, is not a structural policy. That's not a structural policy.

So, I think we have to worry about investments to make our economy more productive and competitive, going forward. Those have to be part of our strategy. It's not just a deficit-reduction strategy.

Senator CASEY. I know we're out of time.

Thank you.

The CHAIRMAN. Thank you.

Senator Shaheen.

And I've been called to a 4 o'clock meeting, so I apologize.

If you—Senator Lugar will close it out. I don't know if he has an additional round that he wants to ask.

But, Senator Shaheen and then Senator Lugar.

And I apologize. I thank the witnesses again.

Dr. TYSON. Thank you.

The CHAIRMAN. There will be questions——

Dr. TYSON. Thank you for the——

The CHAIRMAN [continuing]. For the record. I had some additional questions I wanted to ask you, and I know some other colleagues may want to submit them, so we'll leave the record open, if you don't mind, until the end of the week.

Dr. TYSON. OK, that's fine. Thank you very much——

Ambassador HILLS. Thank you.

Dr. TYSON [continuing]. For the opportunity.

The CHAIRMAN. Thanks.

Senator Shaheen.

Senator SHAHEEN. Thank you.

And thank you both for being here this afternoon.

I would really like to pursue the line of questioning that Senator Casey started with. But, before I do that, I want to ask you—you talked—Dr. Tyson, you talked about the kinds of structural investments and changes we would need to make in this country in order to address some of the challenges that the economy faces. I certainly agree with you, relative to the education and the importance of making sure that a whole strata of people, who are not now getting higher education, need to get that, and the challenges that that encompasses. But, what else do you have in mind when you say that? And I know this is a little off-topic, but you just raised my curiosity.

Dr. TYSON. Well, I personally think we have great innovative strengths in the United States. We still have those. But, I think we have to worry about the fact that we have not kept up our science and engineering talent base. This obviously goes to Senator Lugar's question. This is a very specialized——

Senator SHAHEEN. Right.

Dr. TYSON [continuing]. Talent base that we need to be able to take the basic science support, which we have, and continue to convert it into very successful commercial applications. And I look down the road, and I worry about the fact that there are actually projected shortages of this kind of talent in the near term. We're not talking about 10 years out. We're talking about 5 years out. So, I would put a whole host of things in education.

I personally think that as a transition strategy, but also as a strategy to support competitiveness, going forward we really have a major infrastructure agenda at hand.

And I'm smiling because I just came from a lunch, where a number of people were talking about this. It's been well documented, before the great recession, that the United States was spending significantly less than required to just keep up the infrastructure it had, much less get to world quality standards.

So, if you think about ports and airports and high-speed trains as things that promote competitiveness, they're not just a pleasant journey—they're that, too. I think that's an area of investment which has two characteristics. One, it actually becomes a way to create jobs for these kinds of workers who were in another kind of construction.

And, by the way, I would put energy efficiency investments here. I've been a big supporter of the idea of doing more to promote households to take on energy efficient investments, because those are, basically, residential improvements that require labor to do, but they also achieve another goal.

So, some of the things I think we should be doing are in the infrastructure, energy efficiency, and broadly defined education area. We need to say that we're going to have a different strategy, too, our future is going to look different, too.

Senator SHAHEEN. Thank you.

To go back to China, one of the concerns that I hear from New Hampshire business folks who are thinking about exporting to China is a concern that once their technology—they're working on a new generation of technology, whether it's in solar panels or, you know, Internet, or whatever—Web technology, whatever—that once that technology gets to China, that it's gone, as far as they're concerned. And so, they get the benefit of the first round of exports of whatever that is, but then it's going to get duplicated in China, and they're going to lose their patented technology.

So, how do we address that? Is it through more action at the WTO, or are there other ways in which we can better address China's stealing proprietary technology?

Ambassador HILLS. When any nation fails to take measures to protect our proprietary technology, we should take them to the World Trade Organization. We have an agreement that covers intellectual property. It continues to be a problem in China, although it is improving when compared to a decade or so ago.

China secured a number of patents last year. It moved way up the scale. And when you have a domestic stake in having a system that protects innovation, generally that causes most governments to take a greater interest in developing and enforcing rules to protect intellectual property.

So, we're finding that China is taking a greater interest in protecting intellectual property. But, as they say in China, "the mountains are high and the emperor is far away." And what happens too often at the locality or the province level is not what Beijing wants to have happen. But, we have to keep pushing on that. And I know that some foreign manufacturers are sending their second-tier technology to China because of the very problem that you suggest. So, once again, China's hurting itself.

With respect to all of these issues, it is so clear that opening markets to new ideas is highly beneficial. A government that puts restrictions that keep out inventions and new ideas hurts its own people. And that has been known for a long, long time. But, it is one of the issues that we need to watch carefully and deal with.

I'd like to underscore what Laura Tyson has stated about the infrastructure. You know, in China they have high-speed trains that would take your breath away, literally. And——

[Laughter.]

Ambassador HILLS [continuing]. And that kind of investment adds to a nation's efficiency, cleans up the environment as people pile aboard and don't get into the cars, and creates jobs.

And when we talk about education, yes, we need science and math students to stimulate innovation here at home. So, it's really a great tragedy, in our great Nation that has come so far and once led the world in educating its youth, that today roughly one-third of our high school students fail to graduate. That is simply not tolerable in today's world.

And so, there are a lot of things that we need to do right here at home. Maybe we need a commission on education bringing our teachers unions together with people who deal with educational reform, for the current situation is simply not tolerable. And if we continue down this road, United States tomorrow will not be the same United States today.

Senator SHAHEEN. I couldn't agree more with both of you. I think one of the challenges here has been, How do you reconcile those needs with the deficit and the debt that we have? And—because what you're talking about requires investment, and they're longer term, when we look at the returns on those investments. And so, how do we address the short-term need to respond to this growing debt and deficit that we have?

So, I will just—I'm out of time—but, perhaps after the hearing, could respond to that.

Senator LUGAR [presiding]. Well, thank you very much.

In behalf of the chairman and the members of the committee, I want to thank both of you for wonderful opening statements, which are in the record in full, and for your responses to our questions.

The title of our hearing was "Finding Common Ground With a Rising China," and you have addressed that, and I think members of the committee have, and perhaps increased our understanding, and that of those who are following our hearing.

We will keep the record open, as the chairman suggested, for a few days, for additional questions and your responses.

But, we thank you both very much.

[Whereupon, at 4 p.m., the hearing was adjourned.]

————

ADDITIONAL QUESTIONS AND ANSWERS SUBMITTED FOR THE RECORD

JOINT RESPONSES OF DR. LAURA D. TYSON AND STEPHEN S. ROACH TO QUESTIONS SUBMITTED BY SENATOR JOHN F. KERRY

Question. Where does the Economic Relationship Fit into a Larger Foreign Policy Agenda: What are your views on the importance on the United States—China economic relationship as part of a larger United States-Chinese foreign policy agenda? How has the changing economic relationship altered our broader relationship?

Specifically, are there ways that our economic interdependence constrains U.S. foreign policy options on other issues of concern, such as nonproliferation policy, human rights, Taiwan? Are China's foreign policy options similarly constrained—if so how?

Answer. United States-China economic relationships have been a major focus of the larger United States-China foreign policy agenda during the last quarter century and that will remain the case for the foreseeable future. U.S. policy toward China has been one of engagement rather than containment or competition. The United States has welcomed China as an increasingly prosperous and successful member of the community of nations and has championed China's growing role and responsibilities in global multilateral institutions. And China has embraced economic globalization and has been a reliable global citizen committed to the goals of peace and prosperity. These trends are likely to persist: given the priority of economic growth and development to both its domestic political stability and the legitimacy of its leadership, China has too much to lose to threaten the peace and global economic order on which its growing prosperity depends.

The growing economic links between China and the United States have strengthened the overall relationship between the two nations and have supported their cooperation on many shared interests including promoting global development, addressing global health and environmental challenges, and containing piracy and terrorism.

Both China and the United States have reaped significant economic returns from the large trade and capital flows that link their economies, and both nations have to weigh these returns when they consider how to address areas of disagreement such as nonproliferation policy, human rights, Taiwan and other territorial concerns. In that sense, the foreign policy options of both nations are constrained by their economic interdependence: options that impede the trade and/or capital flows between them would reduce the economic welfare of both of them. That's why both nations should seek to address issues of concerns in other foreign policy areas through bilateral consultation rather than through unilateral confrontation, avoiding economic sanctions to pursue their foreign policy goals in other areas and using multilateral and/or regional institutions and agreements whenever possible.

Question. National Security and the Chinese Economy: Do China's leaders think in terms of national security when they consider the size, composition, pace of development and protection of China's economy? If so, how does this impact their foreign and commercial engagement with the United States and other nations? What is the most appropriate and effective U.S. policy response? What is the best way to pursue our national economic interests and national security interest with China—side by side?

Answer. Despite its dramatic economic progress, China is still a poor country, as measured by its GDP per capita, and confronts large domestic problems including large rural-urban inequalities, a significant pool of underemployed labor in agriculture, and environmental degradation from rapid industrialization. Moreover, the legitimacy of China's authoritarian leadership depends primarily on its ability to deliver rising living standards to its population. For these reasons, China's leaders believe that both China's national security and their political security depend on the growth and development of China's economy: these remain their primary goals and these goals are the primary determinants of their decisions and actions both at home and abroad.

When China joined the WTO, it made significant concessions to liberalize its traditional trade and investment policies as part of its accession agreement. Since that time, China's trade has soared and it has gained significant shares in many global markets. In recent years, China has been relying more on nontraditional barriers such as discriminatory government procurement policies, national standards policies, lax enforcement of intellectual property protection, and local content requirements to boost the competitiveness of its domestic companies. Such practices impede the access of U.S. and other foreign companies to China's domestic market and they are a violation of the spirit and in some instances the law of China's WTO commitments.

The United States should continue to treat such market access barriers as a priority issue in the S&ED trade discussions, should lodge WTO cases against such barriers, and should encourage China's other trading partners to address such barriers in regional and multilateral discussions. The United States should rely as much as possible on multinational, multilateral forums such as the G20, the WTO, the IMF and the U.N. to pursue U.S. economic interests with China and to address bilateral economics disagreements.

Question. China's Treasury Holdings: China's large holdings of U.S. Treasury securities, which totaled $900 billion as of April 2010, make it the largest foreign holder of those securities.

Some U.S. analysts welcome China's purchases of U.S. debt, which help enable the United States to fund its budget deficit and keep U.S. interest rates relatively low. Others have expressed concerns that China's large holdings of U.S. debt could give it significant leverage over the United States. How should we weigh the risks against the benefits?

Answer. China's large purchases of U.S. debt over the last several years have indeed helped to fund the U.S. Federal budget deficit and have kept U.S. and global interest rates lower than they otherwise would have been. These purchases are a reflection of the large and ultimately unsustainable imbalances between saving and investment in both countries. The United States saves too little and consumes more than it produces while China saves too much and produces more than it consumes, relying on the United States and other nations to purchase its excess production. Both countries need to adjust their growth strategies, with the United States relying less on consumption and more on exports and investment to drive growth and China relying more on domestic demand and less on exports. The United States must also adopt a multiyear deficit reduction plan to stabilize the debt to GDP ratio at a sustainable level since dissaving by the U.S. Government is a major contributor to the nation's saving-investment gap.

China has not caused the imbalance between saving and investment in the United States or the fiscal deficit. These are problems resulting from policy choices made at home. To date, the benefits of China's purchases of U.S. Government debt have outweighed the risks. And on economic grounds, China is likely to continue to purchase large amounts of U.S. Government's. But there are risks associated with China's large purchases and holdings of U.S. Government securities. In particular, as we argue in our testimony, even a relatively small decline in China's holdings could be enough to rock global financial markets, triggering a large increase in interest rates and a sharp decline in the dollar's value. China itself would suffer large capital losses on its holdings of U.S. securities as a result. Many observers believe that because of such large potential losses, there is a very low risk that China would use its holdings of U.S. securities to try to influence U.S. policy. In our testimony, we argue that this risk is higher than commonly perceived. For a variety of reasons identified in our testimony, a threat by China to move away from U.S. treasuries in order to change U.S. behavior or in retaliation for U.S. behavior should be taken seriously by U.S. policymakers. Under current financial market conditions, such a threat could trigger investor concerns about the huge financing needs of the U.S. Government, causing a sharp spike in interest rates and a crisis of confidence in U.S. sovereign debt that could cause serious economic harm to both the United States and China.

Question. Competitiveness and U.S. Infrastructure: You mentioned that support for infrastructure investment in the United States was one way to bolster U.S. competitiveness when facing a rising China. Could you please explain to what extent infrastructure investment would reinforce U.S. competitiveness and what needs to happen to ensure adequate infrastructure investment at the pace and scale to ensure U.S. competitiveness in the future?

Answer. A significant and sustained increase in infrastructure investment by Federal, State and local governments should be a priority. Unlike most other forms of stimulus, spending on infrastructure both increases demand when the spending occurs and increases the supply and growth potential of the economy over time The demand-side case for infrastructure investment is well documented. According to the Congressional Budget Office, infrastructure spending is a cost-effective demand stimulus as measured by the number of jobs created per dollar of budgetary cost. Moody's Economy.com estimates that $1 of infrastructure spending increases demand and the level of GDP by about $1.59.

The supply-side or growth case for a significant increase in infrastructure investment is also compelling. Real infrastructure spending is about the same today as it was in 1968 when the economy was a third smaller. The inadequacies of the country's current infrastructure are displayed every day in freight bottlenecks, road congestion, and airport delays, all of which reduce business productivity and make the United States a less attractive location for business activity. Documenting these inadequacies, the American Society of Civil Engineers gave America's infrastructure a failing grade of D in its 2009 report and has identified more than $2.2 trillion in outstanding infrastructure needs. And using a narrower cost-benefit approach, a 2008 CBO study concluded that a 74 percent increase in annual spending on transportation infrastructure alone is economically justifiable.

Over the next 5 years, the Federal Government should work with State and local governments and the private sector to finance $1 trillion of additional investment in infrastructure. The successful Build America Bonds (BAB) program included in the current stimulus package should be extended to support this goal. As part of its commitment to a multiyear infrastructure plan, the Federal Government should also establish and provide the capital for a National Infrastructure Bank. An appropriately designed and governed national infrastructure bank would both address gaps and shortcomings in the current system for selecting and funding infrastructure projects and attract private investment funds for such projects. The bank would focus on transformative projects of national significance, like the creation of a national high-speed rail system or the modernization of the air traffic control system, that require the participation and coordination of many States. Such projects are neglected by the formula-driven processes now used to allocate Federal infrastructure funds among States and regions. The bank would provide both coordination among diverse actors and certainty about the level of Federal funding for such multiyear projects by removing funding decisions from the politically volatile annual appropriations process. Moreover, the bank would select projects for funding, not on political and earmarking considerations that too often influence project selection in the current system, but on independent and transparent cost-benefit analysis by objective experts.

Armed with a flexible set of financing tools, including direct loans, loan guarantees, grants, and interest subsidies for BABs, the bank could provide the most appropriate forms of financing for each project. The bank should be granted the authority to create partnerships with private investors on individual projects. Public-private partnerships would both increase the total amount of funding for infrastructure investments and foster efficiency in project selection, operation, and maintenance. Such partnerships are becoming common in infrastructure financing around the world and many nations are using them to attract private capital, but to date they account for a miniscule share of infrastructure financing in the United States. A national infrastructure bank could tap into the significant pools of long-term private capital in pension funds and dedicated infrastructure equity funds looking for infrastructure investment opportunities.

The Federal Government can afford a capital commitment of at least $25 billion to establish a national infrastructure bank as an additional stimulus measure immediately. Given the significant excess capacity in the economy and the very low interest rates at which the U.S. Government can borrow funds, there is no danger that an additional stimulus of this size will trigger a crisis of confidence in the U.S. Government's creditworthiness. Nor is there any danger that infrastructure investment financed by the bank will "crowd-out" private investment—in fact, it is likely to encourage or "crowd-in" such investment.

As the economy recovers, however, the Federal Government must embark on a multiyear plan to reduce the deficit and stabilize the debt to GDP ratio. To ease capital market anxiety about the Government's future borrowing needs, such a plan should be developed and passed by the Congress now. The plan should include permanent funding mechanisms for the national infrastructure bank. These mechanisms could include a small share of funds from a new multiyear transportation bill, a small share of revenues from the gasoline tax or from a new carbon tax, and user fees. Whenever appropriate and feasible, user fees should be linked to the projects financed by the bank. Such fees would not only raise revenues but would also encourage the efficient use of infrastructure assets and provide financing for their maintenance.

The United States needs to invest significantly more in its infrastructure to secure its competitiveness and deliver rising living standards to its citizens. And there is no better time to begin that investment than now when millions of Americans can be put to work in meaningful jobs to help build the infrastructure we need.

JOINT RESPONSES OF DR. LAURA D. TYSON AND STEPHEN S. ROACH TO QUESTIONS SUBMITTED BY SENATOR RICHARD G. LUGAR

Question. At the hearing, you indicated that the United States needed to make structural economic changes, increase investments in infrastructure, increase education levels and, over the long run, reduce the deficit. In order to support U.S. economic growth and increase employment, what specific structural changes does the United States need to make?

Answer. To reduce its imbalance between saving and investment and its unsustainable current account deficit, the United States must introduce policies to increase national saving and to encourage a shift in the composition of demand away from consumption and toward exports and investment. The most important step is passage of a multiyear deficit reduction policy that stabilizes the debt to GDP ratio at a stable level. This plan should include a major reform of both personal and corporate tax policies to encourage personal saving and business investment. But the plan must also increase government investments in infrastructure, R&D and education. Such investments are essential to boost the competitiveness of the United States as a location for high value-added economic activity and as a source of global exports.

Question. You note in your written testimony that "reducing barriers that impede the access of U.S. companies to China's markets is and should continue to be a major objective of U.S. trade policy." The United States participates in 49 bilateral dialogues with China including economics, trade, politics, energy, and health and engages with China in multilateral for a including the WTO, G20 and United Nations. What more should the United States do to advance our economic objectives with China?

Answer. Reducing nontariff barriers that impede the access of U.S. companies to China's market is and should continue to be a major objective of U.S. trade policy. Given the importance of the government and state-owned companies in China's economy, China's participation in the Government Procurement Agreement (GPA) should be a major objective. The United States should negotiate with China to ease U.S. security controls on U.S. exports to China and to advance the timing for the recognition of China's market economy statues in the WTO (currently scheduled for 2016) in return for a strong offer by China to join the GPA. An agreement along these lines could also help revitalize the Doha Round talks, something that the United States and China committed to do at the last S&ED meetings.

The United States should also take the lead in negotiating a Trans-Pacific Partnership agreement as a first step toward the creation of a free trade area for the Asia Pacific. Several bilateral and regional preferential trading agreements have recently been signed in Asia and the region is heading toward the de facto creation of an economic bloc that would discriminate against the United States. The completion of a Trans-Pacific Partnership agreement would arrest this disturbing trend and could reignite APEC's leading role in global trade liberalization. A revitalized APEC could lead a regional effort for a free trade agreement on green technologies and products.

Question. Too often around the world, the revenues from natural resources are a hindrance to economic and political development. Moreover, conflict over resource revenues can drive price instability and harm supply of oil. In my judgment, promoting transparency is a pivotal need for empowering citizens to ask questions of their governments and hence be empowered to grow economically and democratically. One measure I have offered with Senator Cardin would enhance U.S. leadership by requiring U.S. and foreign companies listed here to disclose their payments to governments as part of Securities and Exchange Commission filings. The importance of U.S. leadership is highlighted with recent mineral discoveries in Afghanistan. China's growing economy also requires oil, gas, and minerals, and at times the government backs their companies' entry into countries. In your assessment, how can we make progress at a governmental and corporate level with China to improve Chinese support for good governance of resources?

Answer. A basic tenet of economics is that market efficiency and competition depend on information, and there is a serious lack of information about the terms of the deals about access to natural resources between governments and private companies. Without such information, there is also ample opportunity for corruption in the decisions by which natural resource rights are allocated. A compulsory disclosure of payments by governments to private interests in natural resource deals is an idea that merits serious consideration.

China and the United States have a common interest in the gains to efficiency and competition and the obstacles to corruption that would result from global or regional agreements that enforce transparency and good governance in natural resource deals between companies and governments. The United States should raise this issue in the S&ED meetings with China and should explore the possibility of cooperating with China to foster a global agreement on this issue within in a multilateral organization like the U.N. or the OECD.

Question. China is currently going through a period of labor unrest and wages are rising in many areas in response. Some American businessmen believe this wage inflation will cascade throughout much of the manufacturing sector. Do you believe this is likely to happen and if so, will Chinese officials find it too much to swallow to also allow their currency to appreciate? In other words would sharply rising wages dampen the pace and size of any currency appreciation? Would the impact on the United States-China trade balance of widespread wage inflation be similar to, or different from, the impact of currency appreciation?

Answer. Contrary to Western press reports, China is not going through a period of labor unrest. The recent increases in wages are a conscious outgrowth of government regulations introduced in 2004, which stipulated that provincial governments increase minimum wages of Chinese workers every other year. During the crisis of 2008–09, when China's export businesses were under severe pressure, those increases—like the currency appreciation policy—were suspended. The gains evident this year were largely a catchup from that hiatus. Even in the aftermath of this latest round of wage inflation, compensation per hour in Chinese manufacturing industries is still only about 4 percent of the comparable pay rate in the United States—hardly a signal that the days of low-cost Chinese labor are numbered. Moreover, total personal income in China is currently only about 42 percent of GDP—less than half the 85 percent reading the United States. In the upcoming 12h Five-Year Plan, the government will make a determined effort to boost the wage share of national income in an effort to raise consumer purchasing power. This policy should not be viewed as an offset to a further, albeit gradual, pace of currency appreciation in the years ahead. However, to the extent that it is part of a proconsumption policy agenda, that will absorb surplus household saving, it can be expected to reduce China's overall current account and multilateral trade surplus. Whether that translates into a smaller bilateral imbalance with the United States, it is equally dependent on actions taken by the United States to boost America's domestic saving rate—necessary to reduce the multilateral trade deficits with China (and, by the way, with 89 other nations) that are an important outgrowth of our unprecedented saving shortfall. A critical first step is passage of a multiyear deficit reduction plan that stabilizes the debt to GDP ratio.

RESPONSES OF AMBASSADOR CARLA A. HILLS TO QUESTIONS SUBMITTED BY
SENATOR JOHN F. KERRY

Question. Where does the Economic Relationship Fit into a Large Foreign Policy Agenda?
- What are your views on the importance of the United States-China economic relationship as part of a larger United States-China foreign policy agenda?
- How has the changing economic relationship altered our broader relationship? Specifically, are there ways that our economic interdependence constrains U.S. foreign policy options on other issues of concern such as nonproliferation policy, human rights, Taiwan? Are China's foreign policy options similarly constrained—if so how?

Answer. It is nearly impossible today to separate our Nation's economic and foreign policy issues. Challenges in one area profoundly affect our ability to be successful in the other, and nowhere is that more apparent than with respect to our relationships with China, the world's fastest growing large economy.

Our Nation's stature as a foreign policy leader requires that we maintain a strong economy. Building a strong economic relationship with China contributes significantly to our Nation's growth and prosperity. Currently China is our third-largest and fastest growing export market. The benefits of our trade opportunities with China have been experienced across America. Virtually every state in the union experienced triple digit increases in exports to China in the decade to 2008, while sales to the rest of the world over the same period grew by just 29 percent. With domestic consumption and investment currently quite weak, strong export growth gives our economy a welcome economic boost.

As two of the world's major players, China and the United States will need to collaborate if we are to deal effectively with a long list of challenges like nuclear proliferation, terrorism, drug and human trafficking, piracy, climate change, and pandemics. It is less that we are constrained by our economic interdependence, and more that our aggregate economic strength provides a means to mobilize the capacity to deal successfully with a growing list of issues that cannot be solved unilaterally in today's globalized world. Indeed, in many instances both China and the United States must collaborate if solutions are to be found.

We will continue to have our differences with China on economic and foreign policy issues as we do from time to time with even our close allies. But we will be better able to bridge those differences and to find solutions that advance the interests of our respective populations by taking actions calculated to build a closer, more candid and constructive bilateral relationship. Taiwan is a case in point. China regards the Taiwan issue as a "core" interest involving its "sovereignty" and believes that we deliberately ignore its sensitivity. Since resuming diplomatic relations with China in 1979, the United States has sought to avoid debating whether Taiwan is part of "one China" but has been clear that Taiwan's future should be decided without the use of force. Our government pledged in the Taiwan Relations Act, also signed in 1979, to provide defensive weapons to ensure that Taiwan could defend itself again an attempt at forceful acquisition. At the present time, the Chinese have an arsenal of missiles in Fujian pointed at Taiwan, and we continue to supply advanced weaponry to Taiwan. The trust among our two militaries lags far behind the trust that exists among our leaders dealing with economic or strategic issues. One could imagine that if we were able to convene a high level and regular Strategic Military Dialogue that it might be possible to reach an understanding whereby China gradually reduced its stock pile of missiles in Fujian and as that positive action occurred the United States delayed sales and downgraded the level of weaponry sold to Taiwan. That sort of deal would require building a much closer and collaborative military-to-military relationship that today does not exist.

Question. National Security and the Chinese Economy
- Do China's leaders think in terms of national security when they consider the size, composition, pace of development and protection of China's economy?
- If so, how does this impact their foreign and commercial engagement with the United States and other nations?
- What is the most appropriate and effective U.S. policy response?
- What is the best way to pursue our national economic interests and national security interest with China—side by side?

Answer. The primary foreign policy goal of the Chinese leadership is to maintain peace at China's borders shared with 14 nations that suffer from varying degrees of instability. China seeks stability in the region and at home so that it can focus on its difficult domestic challenges including existing poverty, income disparity between rural and urban populations, serious environmental concerns including extensively polluted water supplies, foul air and loss of arable land, unemployment, inadequate health care, and a rapidly aging population. Domestically the leadership has made "stability preservation" its top priority. The leadership believes that in order to maintain domestic support it must implement policies that ensure that China's economy continues to grow in ways that will increase prosperity to those who to date have been left behind and to deal with the issues that affect quality of life in China. Over the past three decades in an effort to spur its economic growth, China has opened its markets to foreign investment and reduced its trade barriers, looking to exports and heavy industry to provide the engine of economic growth. Although significant restrictions remain, they are far fewer than existed a decade ago when China joined the World Trade Organization. Overall, the opening of China's markets has both generated domestic economic growth and contributed to global economic growth.

Last year when global growth turned negative and world trade plummeted more than 11 percent, China, along with other nations including the United States, experienced a surge of economic nationalism. Politics in China drove "Buy China" policies just as politics here drove "Buy America" policies, notwithstanding objective economic analysis showed that such policies are detrimental to growth and serve to strain international relations. Bilateral fora like the Strategic and Economic Dialogue and the Joint Commission on Commerce and Trade have been helpful in removing restrictions and building greater understanding. Meetings of leaders and ministers that represent the world's 20 largest economies (the G20), that in total comprise 85 percent of world output and 80 percent of world trade, also provide a useful forum for seeking to reduce trade and investment restrictions. Of course where a particular trade or investment policy is deemed to violate a WTO agreement and negotiation has not resolved the difference, it is appropriate to use the WTO dispute settlement mechanism to resolve the difference, something which both the United States and China have done, thus minimizing potential friction.

In many instances the national economic interests and the national security interests of the United States and China overlap. Both nations want a vibrant global economy that contributes to domestic growth. Similarly both want stability internationally. In some circumstances where we agree on the ends, we differ with respect to the best means to achieve those ends. For example, China and the United States both want to curtail nuclear arms in Iran. China has favored extended diplomacy over sanctions. As a result of our strategic dialogues, China has been willing to support the U.N. resolutions providing for sanctions but has not been willing to support the tighter measures that the U.S. Congress adopted.

In other circumstances we disagree on the risk involved. That is the case with the nuclear ambitions of North Korea. China assesses the risk of North Korea developing an effective nuclear weapon as lower than does the United States. It fears more a collapse of the North Korean Government, worrying it would lead to a flood of North Korean refuges crossing China's north east border causing instability in Liaoning and Jilin provinces and violating China's top domestic policy of "stability preservation." We are more apt to find means to deal with both of our concerns through regular and frequent dialogue. What is missing today is a regular and high-level military dialogue to encourage both sides to better understand the other's risk assessments and to talk about ways to deal with our respective concerns.

Question. China's Treasury Holdings. China's large holdings of U.S. Treasury Securities which totaled $900 billion as of April 2010 make it the largest foreign holder of those securities. Some U.S. analysts welcome China's purchases of U.S. debt which helps enable the United States to fund its budget deficit and keep U.S. interest rates relatively low. Others have expressed concerns that China's large holdings of U.S. debt could give it significant leverage over the United States.

• How should we weigh the risks against the benefits?

Answer. Both those who welcome China's continued purchase of our growing debt and those who express concern over our increasing debt being in foreign hands overlook a critical point. The fact is that there is a serious imbalance in the global economy that has ballooned to unsustainable levels in recent years and puts our future economic stability at severe risk. China, Germany, Japan, South Korea, and other Asian economies have built their growth primarily on exports, whereas the United States, the United Kingdom, and Spain, among others, have relied excessively on domestic consumption, particularly in the housing sector, to fuel their economic growth.

Economists agree that neither of these singly focused growth models is sustainable, and being unsustainable they will change either through gradual policy adjustment or as a result of traumatic financial upheaval.

To protect against future financial crisis will require debtor and creditor nations to adopt more balanced growth plans. Debtor nations cannot continue to consume at the excessive levels of the past, and creditor nations must look more to their own consumers to fuel their economic growth.

Most economists agree that continuing to rely on the growth models of the past decade raises the risk of a crisis to unacceptably high levels. The required changes could constructively be led by the United States, the world's largest debtor nation, and by China, the world's largest surplus nation.

The necessary changes will take time to implement. But it would provide substantial market assurance if the United States and China would publicly lay out a specific 5-to-10-year rebalancing plan at the next meeting of the G20. Each could set forth benchmarks for measuring progress, and provide periodic updates on achievements.

———

RESPONSES OF AMBASSADOR CARLA A. HILLS TO QUESTIONS SUBMITTED BY
SENATOR RICHARD G. LUGAR

Question. You implied that financial and trade protection would have a negative impact on the U.S. economy. Would you please delve into those details on why a rise in protectionism would have bad repercussions? How exactly does protectionism work itself through our economy?

Answer. For the six decades following World War II, under both Democratic and Republican administrations, the United States has led the world in opening global markets. The results have been spectacular. America's policy of seeking to remove barriers to cross border trade and investment has greatly enhanced our Nation's economic growth and the economic well-being of its citizens. As world trade and investment has exploded, standards of living have soared at home and abroad.

A highly regarded economist, Dr. Gary Hufbauer, in a comprehensive study published in 2005 by the Institute for International Economics, now the Peterson Institute for International Economics, calculated that the opening of markets since World War II has increased our Nation's GDP by roughly $1 trillion per year, thus raising the average American household yearly income by $9,500.

Our trade and investment in every region of the world have contributed to this very positive result. Last year when trade plummeted by more than 11 percent, the United States economy contracted by about 2 percent. This year with trade up by 7 percent, the International Monetary Fund is predicting that the U.S. economy will grow by more than 3 percent. With domestic demand and job growth still depressed, external demand is more important than ever.

Unfortunately economic hardship inevitably stokes demands for protection. Yet policies that restrict trade and investment choke off the growth that is especially needed in times of economic adversity. Making matters worse, protectionism is highly contagious. When the United States adopts "Buy America" policies, almost instantaneously our major trading partners, like China, implement a "Buy China" policy. Hence it behooves us to make every effort to explain to the public the harm that results from protectionism and the benefits that flow from opening markets to our products and services.

Dr. Hufbauer's study calculates that the additional opening of world markets to trade and investment would increase U.S. wealth by an additional $500 billion per year, making the average American household richer by an additional $4,500 per year.

It is well documented that jobs connected to international activity earn on average 13 to 18 percent more than jobs in the overall economy. A majority of our exporters are small- and medium-sized businesses that serve as the backbone of America's job creation. The prospects for these businesses and their workers are enhanced by our government's success in the opening of foreign markets.

By ratifying the three pending trade agreements with Panama, Colombia, and South Korea, completing the Trans-Pacific Partnership, and concluding the Doha Development Round the United States could generate additional growth opportunities for the United States and global economies and help keep protectionist impulses at bay.

Question. Your written testimony notes that one way to strengthen U.S. investment ties while ensuring U.S. competitiveness is for the United States to approve the three pending free trade agreements (FTAs) that have been signed with South Korea, Colombia, and Panama. Recently, Senator Kerry and I sent a letter to the administration calling for the Korea-United States FTA to be sent to the Congress for a vote. Also this year, I introduced a resolution in the Senate calling for the administration to develop a framework for FTA negotiations with the Association of Southeast Asian Nations (ASEAN). Over the last 5 years, China has signed nine FTAs including ones with Korea, New Zealand, and the nations of ASEAN. Please describe how U.S. business interests are disadvantaged when competing against China interests in areas where China has an FTA and the United States does not.

Answer. Bilateral and regional free trade agreements are proliferating around the world. The World Trade Organization (WTO) finds there are 262 free trade agreements (FTAs) in force today; the United States is a party to just 17. An additional 100 are currently being negotiated. The United States is negotiating one, the Trans-Pacific Partnership agreement. As a result our entrepreneurs and their workers are disadvantaged vis-a-vis their competitors in countries that have free trade agreements in place which affects our Nation's capacity to grow and to create jobs.

That fact is starkly documented in the World Economic Forum's annual report "Global Enabling Trade" that ranks 125 countries on a range of factors affecting competitiveness. One factor it measures is tariff barriers that impede competitiveness. Chile, as a result of its network of trade agreements, is ranked No. 1, indicating that Chile's exporters face the lowest tariffs globally. The United States with few trade agreements is ranked 114 out of the 125 countries indicating the poor competitive position faced by our exporters. Of course there are many other trade restrictions beyond tariffs that trade agreements alleviate, but the metric on tariffs is illustrative.

The job gains from our trade agreements are substantial. This past May the U.S. Chamber of Commerce released its study "Opening Markets, Creating Jobs, Estimated U.S. Employment Effects of Trade with FTA Partners." Using a general equilibrium economic model, this study examined the 14 FTAs the United States has implemented over the past 25 years, excluding three agreements most recently implemented. It found that 17.7 million U.S. jobs depend on trade with these 14 countries and 5.4 million of these jobs were attributed to the increase in trade resulting from the free trade agreements.

U.S. exporters can lose their competitiveness rapidly when other governments remove trade barriers for their entrepreneurs and our government does not. A study issued on May 10, 2010, undertaken in the House of Representatives by the ranking member of the Ways and Means Committee, the ranking member of the Trade Subcommittee of the Ways and Means Committee, and the ranking member of the Agriculture Committee documented that between 2004–08 Colombia's agriculture market was expanding at 38 percent per year and had become the largest market for U.S. agriculture exports in South America totaling over $4 billion. In 2009, after Colombia entered a free trade agreement with Mercosur, U.S. agriculture exporters' market share in Colombia's agriculture market fell by 31 percent while the market share of competitors from Argentina and Brazil climbed 22 percent. In 1 year American saw their combined sales of corn, wheat, soybeans, and soybean oil plunge 62 percent even as Colombian total imports held steady and to date records show 2010 sales of those products are down 45 percent.

China is the world's largest exporter. It has arranged 14 trade agreements with the 31 economies including 10 nations that comprise the Association of Southeast Asian Nations (ASEAN), is negotiating 5 additional agreements, and is considering negotiations with 2 large economies, India and South Korea.

U.S. competitiveness in the markets where we do not have trade agreements but China does is being adversely affected. It should be noted that the network of agreements that China has and is negotiating in Asia will disadvantage American entrepreneurs in the world's fastest growing region. Sadly, the harm is self inflicted.

Question. Too often around the world, the revenues from natural resources are a hindrance to economic and political development. Moreover, conflict over resource revenues can drive price instability and harm supply of oil. In my judgment, promoting transparency is a pivotal need for empowering citizens to ask questions of their governments and hence be empowered to grow economically and democratically. One measure I have offered with Senator Cardin would enhance U.S. leadership by requiring U.S. and foreign companies listed here to disclose their payments to governments as part of Securities and Exchange Commission filings. The importance of U.S. leadership is highlighted with recent mineral discoveries in Afghanistan. China's growing economy also requires oil, gas and minerals, and at times the government backs their companies' entry into countries. In your assessment, how can we make progress at a governmental and corporate level with China to improve Chinese support for good governance of resources?

Answer. The vast majority of U.S. companies are good ambassadors overseas. In challenging environments they bring American values and demonstrate a positive agenda of corporate social responsibility. Expanding their competitive opportunities will lead to a spread of U.S. values including corporate social responsibility.

The G20 summit meetings provide a multilateral forum where this issue so critical to improving global governance can be discussed beneficially. It is clear that transparency with respect to resource payments to governments would help to limit corruption, enhance global stability, and promote global growth. Leaders of the world's 20 largest economies could agree that they would support transparency with respect to payments made to governments for natural resources by requiring their companies to make such disclosure. The United States could lead by example by adopting the reporting measure that you have suggested.

The Strategic and Economic Dialogue meetings provide a bilateral forum where the United States and China could discuss the benefits that would flow from transparency with respect to resource payments made to governments. An understanding followed by action would give tangible proof of the value of the bilateral dialogue.

Question. China is currently going through a period of labor unrest and wages are rising in many areas in response. Some American businessmen believe this wage inflation will cascade throughout much of the manufacturing sector. Do you believe this is likely to happen and if so, will Chinese officials find it too much to swallow to also allow their currency to appreciate? In other words would sharply rising wages dampen the pace and size of any currency appreciation? Would the impact on the United States-China trade balance of widespread wage inflation be similar to, or different from, the impact of currency appreciation?

Answer. China's 2010 overall inflation rate between January and May ranged between 1.5 percent and 3.1 percent, higher than in 2009 in the midst of the global recession, but considerably lower than in 2008 when the rates between January and May ranged between 7.1 percent and 8.5 percent.

There has been pressure to increase wages in the manufacturing sector. On July 8, Beijing issued its 2010 wage guidelines indicating an average 11-percent salary increase covering both government and enterprise workers. Undoubtedly, Chinese officials will watch closely to see how the higher wage rates affect both growth and inflation.

China's competitiveness will be affected by increases in inflation as well as increases in wages. The benefit of wage increases, if inflation remains under control, is that they will encourages domestic consumption which will help to rebalance China's domestic economy that currently relies too heavily on exports and too little on domestic consumption for growth. Inflation driven by increases in the prices of consumer goods such as housing and food is likely to depress consumption. In recent months China has taken measures to slow the housing boom. There is increased recognition within China's leadership of the need to implement policies so as to stimulate domestic consumption and to reduce those that encourage expansion of heavy industry and exports in order to achieve a more sustainable model for economic growth.

———

RESPONSES OF AMBASSADOR CARLA A. HILLS TO QUESTIONS SUBMITTED BY SENATOR RUSSELL D. FEINGOLD

Question. I have serious concerns regarding past and ongoing human rights abuses in China, including oppression of ethnic and religious minorities, notably in Tibet, and of political dissidents and restrictions on press and assembly, just to name a few. As China continues its economic growth and increases its role on the world stage, what should we expect to see with respect to China's human rights record 10 years from now—positive steps and improvements or a continuation of repression and human rights violations? Is the issue of human rights being adequately addressed in our bilateral engagement, and how can the United States better influence the Chinese on this issue?

Answer. Although it is impossible to predict with any precision the domestic political environment that may exist in any country a decade hence, my hope and expectation is that as China gains the confidence that comes with its enhanced economic security and increased role on the world stage, its leadership will respect widely accepted international norms including those dealing with human rights. China's leadership is increasingly active in international institutions including the United Nations Security Council, the International Monetary Fund, the World Trade Organization, the World Bank, and most recently the G20. All are built on a platform of transparent rules. Only by becoming a "responsible stakeholder" in these organizations can China establish and maintain a global leadership role that I believe its leaders want to achieve.

China's domestic political and social reforms have been much slower in developing than its economic reforms that have transformed the country with unprecedented speed. Still there has been social change since the horrific revolutionary period (1960–1970) of Chairman Mao Zedong. Since 1978 when Deng Xiaoping began the reforms to open China to the world, China's Government has steadily reduced the social and to a lesser extent the political restrictions that the Chinese people faced a generation ago. However I do not see broad support for Western-style democracy in China today where according to numerous polls the vast majority of Chinese believe their government is "on the right track." Nonetheless there is considerable talk among the elite and scholars of the need to enhance pluralism, build an independent judiciary, respect the rule of law, and increase transparency.

Over the past several years reformers in the Central Party School, which serves as the premier training ground for emerging Communist leaders, as well as university scholars have started to debate openly the merits of expanding grassroots political participation, judicial independence, and elections for top party posts. For example, in 2008 Yu Keping, an adviser to President Hu Jintao and Professor and Director of the China Center for Comparative Politics & Economics in Beijing wrote a widely quoted book entitled "Democracy is a Good Thing." Significantly, President Hu in his work report presented to the People Congress in March 2008 urged the Party "to adapt to the growing enthusiasm of the people for participation in political affairs" by expanding grassroots democracy, increasing transparency, and exercising power "under the sunlight to ensure that it is exercised correctly." In "Global Asia," a Journal of the East Asia Foundation, Yu Keping writes in the summer 2010 issue:

> [W]hatever political reforms China carries out, and whatever kind of governance model takes shape in the future, for the country's far sighted leaders the objectives of the governance reform are already irrefutably clear:

democracy, rule of law, fairness, responsibility, transparency, integrity, efficiency, and harmony.

Similarly Zhou Tianyong, senior economist and deputy head of research at the Central Party School stated in a 2008 interview published by the Daily Telegraph: "We have a 12-year plan to establish a democratic platform." He claimed that the government was determined to reform itself, but there had been some infighting between different departments, and he called for the number of ministries to be cut in half to form a "modern government structure" adding "there will be public democratic involvement at all government levels." As support for his positive projection, Professor Zhou said: "There will be many more nongovernmental organizations, chambers of commerce, industry associations and other social groups. Religion should also be given a wider platform to play a positive role. We should protect religious freedom." Although he did not predict the end of the one-party rule, he did state that by 2020 China will basically finish its political and institutional reforms."

People can argue about whether China will achieve those goals. But the fact that Communist Party members within the Party School are publicly talking in these terms indicates that there is some basis to believe that a greater liberalization of politics is underway. This kind of public debate regarding politics represents change for it would not have been permitted a decade ago.

Public lecturing from the outside in my view is counterproductive. Our government can most effectively deal with human rights concerns where it has engaged with China on a broad range of issues of common interest. Working together to solve problems of mutual concern helps to build trust and create relationships that permits candid discussion of differing views and encourages the bridging of differences. There are instances where that has occurred. For example, China joined in denouncing North Korea's nuclear test in 2006, voted to impose and then tighten U.N. sanctions against Iran, supported deployment of U.N.-AU forces to Darfur, condemned the brutal crackdown in Burma, helped in dealing with kidnapping and piracy off the coast of Somalia, and has been constructive in a number of humanitarian efforts. We need to build on our successes. Many of our conflicts occur in areas that involve our militaries. Regular and frequent military dialogues at the highest levels would be helpful in avoiding and resolving a number of our differences.

The private sector can also be helpful. NGOs continue to multiply in China. They are changing public perceptions. Our corporations doing business in China follow high standards that set an example. Also, there are a number of Tract II dialogues that talk about how rule of law, transparency and respect for minority rights contribute to domestic stability and counter corruption, which are objectives given high priority by the Chinese government.

Question. In recent years, China has emerged as a significant economic and political player across Africa. Although Beijing continues to be primarily focused on access to oil and other natural resources, its engagement is matched by significant investments in infrastructure development, without regard to political controversies or concerns about governance or fiscal integrity. I don't think American interests on the continent are necessarily threatened by China's activity, but it is definitely in our interest to pay attention to this activity and consider its long-term strategic implications. How should we address that activity both in our own policy development and in our partnerships with African Governments, particularly given our focus on strengthening good governance and the rule of law?

Answer. China's investment in and trade with sub-Saharan Africa has contributed to a substantial boost in the region's economic growth. China has given aid to most of the countries in the region excepting the few that still recognize Taiwan. Although it began entirely with what some termed "no strings attached" diplomacy which caused concern in the West as Chinese investments and aid went to governments that abused their populations, its policies appear to be evolving. China has positively responded to international pressure.

We can applaud the fact that China's investment both in infrastructure and natural resources have helped to reduce poverty in sub-Saharan Africa. At the same time we can encourage China's active participation in international organizations like the International Monetary Fund and the World Bank that endeavor to advance rule of law, transparency and respect for minority rights. These issues can also be discussed in context of our bilateral dialogues where global stability is an issue of concern to both governments.

Question. For over a decade, China has been Sudan's closest economic partner and its leading trade partner. China purchases about two-thirds of Sudan's exports, and provides one-fifth of its global imports. China is also the leading developer of Sudan's oil industry and a major purchaser of Sudanese oil. While Beijing has reevaluated its relationship with Khartoum in recent years, it continues to be reluctant to press the Government of Sudan on issues related to peace and security. As Sudan moves toward a 2011 referendum on self-determination, constructive engagement from China will be indispensible. What can we expect from the Chinese as we get closer to the 2011 vote and how we can help encourage them to play a productive role within multilateral fora?

Answer. The issues in Sudan are challenging. The April 2010 election resulted in Omar Hassan al-Bashir of the National Congress Party being elected President of the largely Arab-Muslim North and Salva Kiir of Sudan's People Liberation Party elected President of the largely Christian and animist semiautonomous southern region. In accordance with the Comprehensive Peace Accord which ended 21 years of brutal civil war, two referenda will be held on January 9, 2011, to determine whether Southern Sudan will secede and form a new nation and whether Abyei, a region with vast oil reserves, will choose to stay with the North under special administrative status or to join the South which is expected to secede. Intraregional violence has continued in the South amidst allegations that the newly elected government is unable to maintain peace. The head of Sudan's Referendum Commission has warned that Sudan is "alarmingly unprepared" for the referendum. Assuming the referendum proceeds, very tough issues of border demarcation and sharing of oil revenues remain to be decided. Many outside observers have expressed the view that the African Union needs to be more intimately involved. President Thabo Mbeki, Chair of the African Union panel on Sudan, has expressed cautious optimism. The African Union held its summit in Kampala the last week of July to discuss the many daunting pre- and post-referendum concerns.

The United Nations has extended its mission in Sudan. In late July United Nations representatives met with representatives of the African Union and expressed a willingness to work with the Sudanese Government and the international community to ensure a free and credible referendum. China, a member of the Security Council, has voiced support for the referendum and a strong desire for stability in the region where it has substantial investments. Since 2007, it has increased its support of international peacekeeping missions and there is no indication that China will alter its current policy either before or after the referenda. What actions the two governments take after the referenda will depend on the facts on the ground and future actions would be an appropriate subject for our bilateral strategic dialogue.

Question. Are we paying enough attention to Chinese attitudes toward the United States—both those of Chinese citizens and those of the political and military establishments? There have been some troubling press stories on this issue—for example a survey conducted for the Sunday Times of London of Chinese-language media found "army and navy officers predicting a military showdown and political leaders calling for China to sell more arms to America's foes." Similarly, the Washington Post reported earlier this year poll results indicating that many in China see the United States as "the No. 1 threat to China's rise." Should we be doing more in the way of public diplomacy to China?

Answer. There are misperceptions in both China and the United States about the other. Many in China, not only in the leadership and media but also ordinary citizens, see the United States as seeking to limit China's reemergence as a global leader. At the same time many Americans including some Members of Congress and the media talk about China as "tomorrow's enemy," which feeds China's misperceptions regarding the United States and undercuts efforts to build a closer, more candid, and collaborative bilateral relationship. That is why engagement at high levels, public and private, is critical. Public diplomacy in China can be helpful. But we need to take steps here at home. It would be helpful if more of our leaders were to state publicly that they want to establish a closer, more candid, and collaborative bilateral relationship and to inform their fellow Americans about why and how China is important to U.S. future prosperity and security. Most Americans are unaware that China is our fastest growing export market and our third-largest customer behind Canada and Mexico. Many Americans complain that China limits our inward investment and take that as a hostile act, but are unaware that recently 50 Members of Congress have expressed opposition to China's Anshan Iron & Steel Group making a 20-percent investment in U.S. Steel Development Co., a small plant in Mississippi, that would bolster a U.S. company and create U.S. jobs. Many Americans see as evidence of protectionism China's procurement policies that seeks to limit government high technology purchases to "indigenous" products, but do not see our Buy America" restrictions as a rough equivalent. With a better informed public, we would be in a better position to build a stronger bilateral relationship that would benefit both sides.

○